A History of

CLEVELAND'S
PLAYHOUSE
SQUARE

A History of

CLEVELAND'S
PLAYHOUSE
SQUARE

MICHAEL R. ROUTA

THE
History
PRESS

Published by The History Press
Charleston, SC
www.historypress.com

Front cover, top, left to right: "Thank You Playhouse Square," author photo, 2021; "Palace Theater Marquee just prior to closing," *Cleveland Press* photographer, Tom Prusha, Cleveland Memory Project, Cleveland State University; "Mr First Nighter," *Cleveland Press* photographer, Bernie Noble, Cleveland Memory Project, Cleveland State University; *bottom*: Playhouse Square chandelier, Aerial Agents of Seven Hills, Ohio.
Back cover, left to right: The Lumen, author photo, 2021; sign outside Loew's State going down, *Cleveland Press* photographer, Bill Nehez, Cleveland Memory Project, Cleveland State University.

First published 2021

ISBN 9781540249180

Library of Congress Control Number: 2021938380

This book is dedicated to the many volunteer Redcoats who give of their time to create a most enjoyable theater experience for those attending performances at Cleveland's Playhouse Square. It is also dedicated to the volunteer tour guides who make time in their busy lives to research and keep alive the stories and histories of the theaters. It is also dedicated to the Playhouse Square Foundation staff (past and present) who plan and provide performances and operate and protect Playhouse Square for future generations to experience and appreciate.

CONTENTS

Preface   9
Acknowledgements   11

1. Cleveland's Theater Roots   13
2. Turn of the Century and Foundations of Playhouse Square   21
3. Architects, Builders and Buildings   31
4. Opening Nights   52
5. Music, Musicians and Movies   58
6. First Theater Managers   62
7. Changing Entertainment Options   70
8. Welcome Mr. First-Nighter   79
9. A Tale of Two Anniversaries   88
10. Rebirth   97
11. Volunteers   131
12. The Future and the Next One Hundred Years   134

Bibliography   139
About the Author   141

PREFACE

I n 1921 and 1922, Playhouse Square in Cleveland, Ohio, opened the second-largest concentrated collection of theaters in the country outside of New York City. Thanks to some serendipitous events, luck and the energy and vision of individuals in Cleveland, that description still holds true today. Although the city has changed greatly since the 1920s, the theaters in Playhouse Square shine brightly and amaze audiences, much as they did when they first opened one hundred years ago.

The theater works because of good storylines, building tensions, unsure endings and great performances by a cast and company. The story of Playhouse Square contains all of those elements. The story told in this book focuses on the cast and company of characters who built the theaters, worked in the theaters and saved the theaters. In a good Broadway show, it is the cast that draws us in and keeps us interested. Great theaters are built by characters of vision and decorated in scenery that is a feast for our eyes. There are backstories and foreshadowing episodes. In a well-crafted show, the cast contains stars and minor characters, but each person is needed to move the story along. Characters make things interesting and bring life to the stage.

Over the next several pages, we will be introduced to the people who had the idea of creating a Playhouse Square. We will meet the builders who supplied the money to build these wonderful showplaces. We will also meet the players who had a vision of what makes a showplace and how to save one. There were managers who worked to keep the places running and advertised to build an audience. In desperate times, there are also heroes and civic leaders who contribute time and money in equal measure. There are countless volunteers and next-gen adults who develop business plans to ensure that future theatergoers will be able to appreciate classic theaters and excellent showmanship. All of it is played out within the context of community and national events that impact the stories told not only on the stage but also about the theaters themselves.

Our journey begins with the everyday work of key individuals who were interested in making a living and creating entertainment venues that would surprise and amaze. In Cleveland's case, some of the cast were from out of town, arriving as a road show and passing through to the next stop. Others were homegrown actors who had a vision and were looking for a local legacy. The story begins at the end of the nineteenth century, with the roots of Cleveland theater, and continues for more than one hundred years. Sit back and enjoy the story.

Acknowledgements

I n 2014, I retired from work as a special-education teacher, school administrator and adjunct professor. As with most retirees, my life did not end when work ended. Like many Clevelanders, I am Cleveland-centric, and I wanted to give something back. Growing up in Cleveland and fondly remembering family outings to Playhouse Square, I investigated ways to help out at Playhouse Square Center.

It was in becoming a Redcoat that my excitement about the theaters grew exponentially. I met a fellow Redcoat, Joe Ferritto, a head usher who often spoke about conducting behind-the-scenes tours of the theaters. Joe nominated me to become a tour guide and, once I accepted, mentored me through the process of learning the history and stories about Cleveland's wonderful theaters. Tom Rathburn, Don Fedorchak and Barb Mazzone shared many stories and anecdotes about their years as tour guides and Redcoats during breakfast gatherings prior to Saturday tour dates or over lunch after the tours.

My interests in the people who were important to the Conner Palace, Key Bank State, Mimi Ohio. Allen and Hanna Theaters engaged my spare time as I researched each theater's history. My initial goal of the research was to become a better tour guide. However, I realized that many of the stories were spread across many resources and were difficult to find. Ruth Flannery, from Playhouse Square Foundation, allowed me to view the archives of the foundation and encouraged my curiosities about the people who conducted business at the theaters. Frank Dutton, John Hemsath and Lawrence Wilker were all patient and gracious with their time in answering questions I had about each theater and their roles in protecting them. John and Lawrence were especially helpful in filling in the blanks regarding the backstories as the theaters were being reborn and Playhouse Square Foundation was growing.

Thanks also to Aerial Agents of Seven Hills, Ohio, for sharing their wonderful photo of the Playhouse Square chandeliers on the cover of this book.

I can only hope that in some small way my efforts keep the history alive and promote continued interest and success in the second-largest theater group in the country, the largest theater reconstruction center and the magnificent five theaters that make up Cleveland's Playhouse Square.

1

CLEVELAND'S THEATER ROOTS

JOHN ELLSLER

The initial links to Playhouse Square started in 1853, when John Ellsler bought the Cleveland Theater. The theater, located on Bank Street (now West Sixth), was a struggling showplace. By starting and organizing the city's first stock company, Ellsler began the march toward Playhouse Square. He also opened an actor's school as part of his company of actors. He worked hard to create respectability for the theater and the actors in his adopted home. Perhaps no one person did more to advance the image and success of theater in the city of Cleveland between 1860 and 1875.

John Ellsler arrived in Cleveland by way of Baltimore and Philadelphia. He was born in Harrisburg, Pennsylvania, in 1821 and moved to Baltimore to work in a print shop. The shop produced programs and posters for theaters. It was while delivering the printed material to the theaters around town that Ellsler gained his first interest in performing.

By 1843, he had returned to Philadelphia and was working as the assistant treasurer of Peale's Museum. In the 1840s, a museum was not only a place where a visitor could view paintings and artifacts from afar but also could be entertained with lectures and curiosities. The contents of Peale's Museum were purchased by P.T. Barnum in 1849 and were used as part of the exhibits for his American Museum in New York.

In 1846, John Ellsler became a member of the Arch Street Theater in New York and then moved on to the Chatham Street Theater. It was while at the Chatham Street Theater that he met and married Euphemia Emma Myers, an actress at the theater. In 1849, the couple's travels brought them to Cleveland. While in Cleveland, John and his wife performed at the Foster's Varieties.

He soon settled in Cleveland and became the manager and a performer at the Cleveland Theater. The theater was on the third floor of a building on Bank Street opposite the Johnson Block. The theater had a forty-foot stage and an auditorium reported to hold two thousand patrons. It opened in April 1855 and was one of several competing showhouses in the city at that time. In time, the Cleveland Theater was renamed the Academy of Music. It was not only the center of theater life in Cleveland but also an actor's school that developed performers and hosted national traveling artists.

Among the artists who performed at the Academy of Music was John Wilkes Booth in December 1863. John Ellsler knew Booth and found himself being interviewed by federal authorities soon after Booth shot Abraham Lincoln. Ellsler was not under suspicion for long, but knowing Booth and being briefly connected to Lincoln's assassin, no matter how remote, surely must have caused Ellsler some anxiety.

As the success of the Academy of Music grew, so did the interest in theater by Cleveland's most fashionable. The success of industrialists in oil, iron ore and shipping brought great wealth and, with that, a refinement in pastime activities. Euclid Avenue grew after the Civil War into one of the most fashionable and well-regarded streets in the world. The audiences at the academy also grew, and John Ellsler began considering a new theater—a theater that would be one of the finest in the country.

Supported by Jeptha H. Wade, Horace Weddell and A.W. Fairbanks (all members of Cleveland's moneyed elite), Ellsler invested his own money in the construction of the Euclid Avenue Opera House. The development of the opera house came about in 1873. Early in the planning, the building was to have two entrances. The main entrance of the opera house was built on Sheriff Street (now East Fourth) and had a tunnel connected to an entrance on Euclid Avenue. The Euclid entrance allowed patrons to be dropped off on the avenue and enter the theater's lobby (thus providing access to Euclid and lending the name to the theater). The panic of 1873, a result of speculative investments primarily by railroads and inflation, slowed construction. This delayed the opening until 1875, as additional investors had to be lined up to complete the project. This foreshadowed issues that would impact the opera house within a few years.

In September 1875, the long-awaited opening of the Euclid Avenue Opera House took place under the lessee of Ellsler. The opening night featured a performance of *Saratoga*. Ellsler and his wife, Euphemia, as well as

The Euclid Avenue Opera House was conceived by John Ellsler and opened in 1875. It was bought by Mark Hanna at auction. *Courtesy of Cleveland Memory Project. Playhouse Square Archives Collection.*

their daughter Effie, all had leading roles. The *Plain Dealer* praised the new theater as a "lasting monument to the enterprise and spirit of the citizens of Cleveland." The crystal gas chandeliers, imported marble and velvet interior provided an elegant look for the theatergoers from Euclid Avenue.

The opera house, which could seat 1,600 patrons, cost an estimated $200,000, with nearly $12,000 in overruns connected to the delay in construction. The theater brought in large crowds throughout the late 1870s, but John Ellsler was a better actor and teacher than he was a financial manager. Money was the backbone of the industry; as such, running a theater was expensive, especially since the prevailing tastes of the day were moving from local stock companies to touring companies. John Ellsler's stock company was large; it included thirty actors and more than twenty support staff. As touring companies began arriving in Cleveland at the opera house, Ellsler had to lease back the Academy of Music to supply work and training for his stock company. His finances became overextended, and debt began to rise.

MARK HANNA

Mark Hanna was a member of Cleveland's industrial class. His family moved to Cleveland in 1852 from Lisbon, Ohio, where he had graduated from Central High School. After leaving Western Reserve College, he entered the family's grocery business. He married Charlotte Rhodes and, after some failed attempts on his own, entered her father's iron and steel business. In partnership with others, Hanna created a diversified company that handled coal, iron ore and steel products. Along the way, he was an owner of the *Cleveland Herald*, an unsuccessful newspaper that eventually was closed and sold to its competitor. He also entered banking and established the Union National Bank. He remained president of the bank until his death.

Mark Hanna enjoyed the better things in life, and he enjoyed going to the theater. The story as to how he ended up owning a theater is one of impulse and lore. Hanna was coming down Euclid Avenue after lunch one afternoon when he and his companions noticed a commotion on Sheriff Street. A sheriff's sale was being conducted to sell the Euclid Avenue Opera House. They wandered into the sale. As the bidding proceeded, the sale approached $40,000. On impulse, Hanna made an offer, and a deal was concluded. He was now the owner of the opera house, and his family's connection to a future Playhouse Square was sealed.

Abraham Erlanger was business manager at the Euclid Avenue Opera House and in the 1890s created a theatrical syndicate controlling bookings and contracts. *Wikimedia file: Abraham Lincoln Erlanger.*

Hanna was not an active owner when he took over the Euclid Avenue Opera House in 1879, instead turning the management of the theater to a relative, L.G. Hanna. This did not work out, and Mark was forced to look elsewhere for a new manager. Enter Augustus Hartz, born in Liverpool, England, and a traveling magician for close to twenty years. He settled in Cleveland due to an offer by Jeptha Wade to manage part of his property portfolio. Hartz was never far from theater, and when the Park Theater (located on the northwest corner of Public Square) needed a manager, he was persuaded to take the position. The newly built Park Theater was advertised as the only fireproof auditorium in the country. It burned down in January 1884, and Augustus Hartz moved on to the Euclid Avenue Opera House, working for Hanna.

Gus Hartz was a skilled manager. His success at the Euclid Avenue Opera House lasted until the theater was closed in 1920. Starting in 1884, he was not only the manager but also the lessee. Hartz made the venue a successful concern, and it became the most popular theater in Cleveland. Only the building of the new theaters on Playhouse Square and investment of the Hanna family in the new Hanna Theater caused the opera house to lose favor with patrons.

Another person whom Hanna acquired at the Euclid Avenue Opera House was Abraham Lincoln Erlanger. He started out working in an opera-glass stand and the cloakroom. He became head usher and helped out backstage, eventually working in the ticket booth. Under Hanna, Erlanger became the treasurer and business manager. He was born in Buffalo, New York, but spent his formative years in Cleveland. After leaving the opera house, he entered into a partnership with Marc Klaw, a Kentucky lawyer. He recognized that an organized process of booking acts and scheduling them between cities was needed to bring stability and consistency to theatrical concerns. Erlanger and Klaw created a theatrical syndicate in 1896. This syndicate grew into a network that controlled every aspect of contracts and bookings in the United States.

B.F. Keith and Edward Albee

About the time Hanna and Hartz were solidifying the status of the Euclid Avenue Opera House, Benjamin Keith was opening up his first dime museum in Boston. Keith created a partnership with Edward Albee that would forever change vaudeville, and Albee would eventually end up building the Palace Theater in Cleveland.

Born in 1846, Benjamin Franklin Keith was the youngest of eight children. At the age of sixteen, he ran away to the circus, worked with P.T. Barnum and got a job with Brunnell's Museum in New York City. Edward Franklin Albee also took off for the circus and worked as a tent boy and became a ticket broker. Albee spent seven years in the circus.

In 1885, Keith opened the Gayety Museum in Boston, a dime museum featuring prematurely born infant "Baby Alice." As Baby Alice outgrew the role, Keith looked for another means to continue his museum. In 1886, he needed an influx of money and partnered with Albee. The two had the idea to clear out the second floor of the Gayety to present variety acts. It was

Left: B.F. Keith expanded vaudeville and created the Keith Vaudeville Circuit, offering "big time" vaudeville throughout the East Coast. *Wikimedia file: Benjamin Franklin Keith*.

Right: Edward Albee was B.F. Keith's partner and the driving force behind the Keith organization's building and owning large deluxe theaters. *Wikimedia file: E.F. Albee*.

Albee who cleaned up the lower museum floor and set up the continuous-shows format upstairs. The Gayety was such a success that they leased the Bijou Theatre next.

Back in Cleveland, a new theater was being built with the financial support of Charles H. Bulkley. Charles was father to Robert Bulkley, whose company built the Bulkley Building that houses the Allen Theater on Playhouse Square today. In 1885, the Cleveland Theater opened under the management of Frank Drew, but within the year, Drew left the theater and H.R. Jacobs took over. Jacobs changed the name to Jacob's Theater, and it remained the name until the theater burned down in 1891.

John Ellsler returned to manage the reopened Park Theater after it was rebuilt in 1886, but within a single season, the Park was closed again. He left Cleveland in 1886, never to return after that last season as manager of the Park.

In Boston, Keith and Albee were churning out Gilbert and Sullivan shows, all pirated versions, and were making a great deal of money at the Bijou. They were making so much money that the pair began opening other theaters along the East Coast, all using the same format. In 1887, they opened a theater in Providence; in 1889, a theater in Philadelphia; and, in 1893, the Hippodrome Theater in New York at Times Square.

It was Albee, helped by Keith's wife, Mary, who arranged financing from the Diocese of Boston to build a "deluxe" theater. Albee assured the diocese that all shows would be absent profanity and rigidly censored. They in fact were building on the work of Tony Pastor, also a former circus man, who cleaned up variety shows in the earliest days of vaudeville. It was at this point that Albee began exerting greater control over the Keith-Albee Theatrical Corporation. The Boston Colonial opened in 1893 and was the first of many "deluxe" theaters that Albee built on behalf of the Keith Theatrical Corporation.

The Keith-Albee organization controlled theaters in many cities along the East Coast at the turn of the century. Performers who were under contract with Keith Theatrical would move from city to city, following a circuit that limited the distance between performance stops. Albee was the general manager of the Keith circuit and, by 1900, was head of an organization called the United Booking Office, which hired performers for the circuit.

2

TURN OF THE CENTURY

AND FOUNDATIONS OF

PLAYHOUSE SQUARE

A t the start of 1900, Cleveland was a bustling and growing city. Euclid Avenue was considered one of the most beautiful avenues in the country, if not the world. Cleveland's population was growing along with its wealth. In 1900, Cleveland was the seventh-largest city in the country, and many industrial leaders called it home. There was a recognition on the part of Cleveland's wealthy that philanthropy and investment in the city should be part of their civic duty.

The major families began to create endowments for current consumption and future posterity. Mark Hanna, Jeptha Wade, Samuel Mather and John Huntington used their wealth and political influence to expand the city's cultural impact. The success of those efforts laid the groundwork for enormous growth in cultural institutions and the expansion of access for everyone in Cleveland.

Mark Hanna directed much of his energy toward politics. He was instrumental in supporting William McKinley's successful presidential campaign and was himself appointed to the U.S. Senate in 1896. Mark Hanna died in 1904, but the Hanna family continued to have an interest in the Euclid Avenue Opera House. The theater was a financial success, and patrons filled the seats regularly.

In 1900, the city had four theaters available to residents, but by 1904, nine theaters were open, providing a range of entertainment options for all classes of patrons. This unprecedented growth led the *Cleveland Plain Dealer* to describe the city as ranking high among the "good show towns." The options for patrons were diverse and included "one [theater] devoted entirely to first class traveling productions, one to light opera, two to vaudeville, one each to popular priced productions, stock productions, melodrama and burlesque." The varied options and continued success of these theaters was making people outside of the city take notice.

The same year, 1904, saw B.F. Keith begin expressing interest in opening a theater in Cleveland. He was looking to either build a theater or buy one to add to his circuit. Edward Albee had recently created the United Booking Office and he successfully limited an attempt by performers to unionize, thus establishing a booking trust. Keith had also recently opened a $1 million theater in Pittsburgh and was about to start building a vaudeville house in Buffalo. Cleveland was the next logical place to add to his circuit.

Joseph Laronge

Cleveland was putting up buildings and homes to serve the growing population and continued business needs. The city was extending out from the central city area with new suburbs and outlying areas, developed for people to live and work. The city was ripe for real estate development, and in 1903, an enterprising young real estate salesman opened an office in the newly completed Williamson Building.

Joseph Laronge, the "Father of Playhouse Square," was born in 1881 and began working in real estate with the Frisble Company and later helped to organize the Bingham-Jackson Company. In September 1903, he and his brother A.L Laronge opened their real estate and brokerage company, which would also have a claims adjustment department.

The *Plain Dealer* regularly had real estate advertisements, and the success and growth of the Laronge Realty Company can be tracked, in some measure, through the number and type of listings printed in the paper. Tracking the advertisements shows a growth through the early years of the 1900s, as both the company and the city were booming. The Laronge Realty Company grew from a modest 15 sales advertisements in 1904 to 241 by 1912. In addition to the increase in the number of realty offerings listed by the company, the type of listings during that period expanded to include lots, rental units, homes, apartment buildings and industrial sites throughout the Cleveland area. The value of the properties listed ranged from a few hundred dollars to tens of thousands of dollars. The company handled real estate on the east side, west side and suburbs.

Marcus Loew

In 1904, Marcus Loew started a penny arcade in New York, the People's Vaudeville Company. Born in 1870 in New York, Marcus Loew was an ambitious young man. By the time he turned twenty-three, he had worked in various businesses and lost several ventures. Around that age, he met David Warfield and Adolph Zukor and was introduced to the arcade business. Zukor had established the Automatic Vaudeville Company in 1903. (Zukor would eventually start Paramount Pictures Corporation.) The arcade business was a group of coin-operated machines that played music, tested a person's strength and flashed thirty-second photoplays, often using a machine known as a Mutoscope. Penny arcades were wildly successful, and working-class immigrants became fascinated with the moving pictures in the single-reel machines.

Marcus Loew's investment in the People's Vaudeville Company was so successful that, within a year, he had opened four more arcades throughout New York City. The next logical step was to create viewing rooms. In 1907, Loew rented a space in Cincinnati for a nickelodeon. These venues, called nickelodeons because the price of admission was five cents, allowed groups of people to sit in seats and watch a photoplay projected on a white screen or sheet. The public was already interested in penny movie arcades, where patrons stood and watched the moving pictures for thirty seconds. In a nickelodeon, the paying public could sit and watch several reels during one performance. Again, the attraction was very successful, so much so that Loew remodeled an old vaudeville theater and renamed it the Royal.

The Royal offered a mix of films and vaudeville acts. Combining the two forms of entertainment allowed Loew to charge more than a nickel (usually ten or twenty-five cents), but not as much as a patron would pay to see a regular vaudeville show. It was the start of a successful business, allowing Loew to make connections with the Shubert vaudeville and legitimate theater organizations. Using a mix of film and "low vaudeville," Marcus Loew was able to sidestep a confrontation with B.F. Keith and Edward Albee's vaudeville trust, allowing the Loew's Theatrical Enterprise to expand and grow. This mix of movies and live vaudeville was Loew's signature programming in his theaters and remained that way for his entire career.

In 1906, two other young men were finding success in the photoplay business. Jay and Jules Allen opened a Theatorium with their father in Pennsylvania. The Allen brothers looked at the growing competitive landscape of movies and determined that they would have more success if they took their ideas to Canada. In 1908, they established the Allen Amusement Corporation and built their first Allen Theater in Calgary.

B.F. Keith opened his first Cleveland vaudeville house in 1904 after several starts and stops. Late in 1903, there was speculation that he would buy the Star Theater from a Mr. Drew in a deal that would also have Drew take over the Colonial Theater. Then, in the spring of 1904, B.F. Keith was reported to be looking at buying property in which to build a new theater, one that would be equal to or rival the one he built in Buffalo. He actually ended up buying the Prospect Theater from Augustus Hartz. In addition to being the lessee and manager of the opera house, Hartz was the owner of the Prospect Theater.

Keith was gambling that Cleveland would be able to support two vaudeville theaters: the Empire, under the management of John Drew; and the newly purchased Prospect Theater. A stock company was performing at the Prospect but closed, and the theater was remodeled. The *Plain Dealer* thought the entertainment public would reap the benefits of having two vaudeville houses vie for their patronage.

B.F. Keith's presence in Cleveland was just beginning. In December 1908, his organization bought the giant Hippodrome Theater and retained ownership of the Prospect Theater. The footprint of the Hippodrome, which opened in December 1907, went from Euclid to Prospect Avenues and included a 13,500-square-foot stage. The stage was divided into four sections, each of which could be independently raised four stories. The "Hipp" was designed to show spectacles with a large number of actors and animals and had a water tank below the stage.

The Hippodrome was to have two office buildings erected above the auditorium, but cost overruns delayed the completion of the eleven-story building facing Euclid and a seven-story building on Prospect. The business plan was to have the office space in the building offset the costs of running the theater. It was a good plan, but the fact that those two buildings were neither completed nor rented out when the theater opened placed the Hippodrome in financial difficulties.

Five months after the theater opened, it went into receivership. The bidding to reopen the theater was among the Shubert Theater organization, William Morris vaudeville booking, two movie theater owners and the Keith Theatrical Organization. Keith won over the other bidders.

Keith immediately set his mark on the decor of the theater. He added oriental rugs and oil paintings. Under the stage, he set up a manufacturing and learning center to be used by vaudeville performances. The center included a scenery shop, a place to make costumes and training rooms for singers and dancers. The workshop was used for the complete Keith circuit.

Besides vaudeville performers from around the country, Keith booked Sunday movies. Many were travel movies and an occasional full-length movie. Sometimes, the films were shown between vaudeville performances. He used Albee's United Booking agency to lock in vaudeville performers and lock out those that were not signed to United Booking. Other theaters in Cleveland found it difficult to bring in major and well-known acts due to Keith and Albee's aggressive tactics.

Joseph Laronge continued to build his business as Keith's Theatrical Organization was building a footprint in Cleveland. As of 1910, Laronge's company moved into more spacious offices in the Williamson Building, and in 1911, he was a part of the incorporation of a newly formed, additional realty company, Sixth City Realty. Sixth City Realty had four other partners, and the new company was incorporated with an initial investment of $15,000.

Additionally, in 1911, Laronge was associated with the sale of the Princess Theater, located on Euclid Avenue near the public square. The transfer was to a group owning the Corona Theater on Prospect Avenue and East Ninth Street. One can only speculate as to whether this was the beginning of an interest in entertainment venues for Laronge. What is known is that Laronge was becoming very successful, and his property interests were increasing.

In 1910, B.F. Keith's first wife, Mary, died, and Keith went into retirement as a multimillionaire. He officially turned over the operations of the company to his son Andrew Paul and to Edward Albee. Albee was for all practical purposes running the day-to-day operations and the vaudeville acts through United Booking Office, and he was building and leasing theaters around the country in Keith's name.

Keith died four years later, in 1914, while on his honeymoon to his second wife, Ethel Chase. Ethel was forty-one years younger than Benjamin. When Keith died, she received a handsome estate, but the bulk of the company was already in the hands of Andrew Paul (who died as a result of the Spanish flu in 1918) and Edward Albee.

Marcus Loew was also increasing his business starting in 1910. As of that time, Loew owned and operated theaters throughout New York City. In an effort to expand his holdings and increase his influence, he created Loew's Consolidated Enterprises. He received financial support from the Shuberts, who invested $200,000 in the new company. He also continued his relationship with Adolph Zukor, who became the company's treasurer.

Marcus Loew was president, and the influx of capital allowed him to further expand his theatrical holdings.

Within a year, Loew's Consolidated Enterprises gave way to a new company, Loew's Theatrical Enterprises. He was also making moves into the movie industry through a company that acquired movies and then distributed them to other theaters, charging them rent: film by the foot. In 1914, Loew's Theatrical Enterprises had a major expansion, buying up a competing theatrical syndicate and gaining thirty theaters in the Midwest and on the West Coast. The expansion provided Loew with a consistent flow of talent within his own circuit, and the formula of live entertainment and movies continued.

The expansion also secured Loew's financial stability, because he owned the theaters where his "small-time" vaudeville circuit and movies played. He did venture into theaters that focused mainly on movies as well. His continued relationship with Adolph Zukor was proving beneficial, because Zukor was moving quickly into the motion picture business, creating the Famous Players Film Company and a distribution company called Paramount Pictures. This vertically integrated production and distribution company also controlled some of the best-known movie actors in the country.

The Allen brothers were enlarging their own theater group and gained the franchise in Canada for Paramount Distribution. Among the stars that Zukor's Paramount and Famous Players Film Company had under contract was Mary Pickford. Pickford, born in Toronto, was the most popular star in movies starting in 1914. Using the exclusive rights to exhibit Pickford films in Canada, the Allen brothers' theaters grew to a chain of over one hundred movie houses. Their success allowed them to envision expanding theaters into the United States. They had eyes on two cities in particular: Detroit and Cleveland.

As Marcus Loew was growing his Theatrical Enterprise company and venturing further into motion pictures, so too was Joseph Laronge. In 1915, Laronge, working with three partners—Louis Becht, Fred Desberg and Edward Strong—incorporated the Mall Theater Company with a $150,000 capitalization. This firm built the Upper and Lower Mall Theater complex. The Mall Theater, on Superior Avenue, actually opened in 1909. The theater got entangled in a political controversy when the manager, Louis Becht, was arrested three times between 1909 and 1915.

The new theater complex took advantage of the elevation differences between Superior and Euclid Avenues to create two main floors. It was described in the *Plain Dealer* as "unlike any other theater building in the

United States." The Mall Theater complex may well have been the first duplex theater in America. One theater was just above the other, and a marble staircase connected the venues.

The total seating for the two theaters was fifteen hundred. There were six hundred seats in the Lower Mall and nine hundred seats in the Upper Mall. When the showhouses opened, both played movies, albeit of different lengths. The Lower Mall, which had an entrance on Superior Avenue, presented two-reel films. These films were mostly comedies, travel films, newsreels and short subjects. The Upper Mall played first-run movies and five-reel films featuring stars and big-time attractions.

Keith Theatrical Enterprises was by now clearly and fully under the control of Edward Albee. He consolidated his hold on vaudeville performers through blacklisting and banning actors who continued to support the White Rats (a performers' union competing against United Booking). In fact, he actually bought out the union clubhouse for the White Rats when the organization went bankrupt and created a new organization, the National Vaudeville Actors (NVA). The NVA took over the Rats building and membership rolls and operated as a managers' union supporting the United Booking Office. Both of these organizations were controlled by Albee.

With the performers under control, Albee turned his attention to building theaters of grand proportions and style. He was becoming more involved in the details of creating deluxe vaudeville show palaces along the East Coast and in the Midwest. These theaters were even more elegant and extravagant than those Keith oversaw when he was alive. Many were built to honor B.F. Keith, and all were operated under the Keith Theatrical Organization name.

The Allen brothers continued to build movie houses and made plans to build two theaters in Cleveland. The first was to be part of the planned Bulkley Building to be constructed on Euclid Avenue and Fourteenth Street. The second was to be built on the west side at Gordon Square.

Laronge now joined forces with Marcus Loew and established the Loew's Ohio Theaters Company. Laronge was the vice-president of the company, and with the financial backing of the Loew's Theatrical Enterprise, he began to assemble a collection of theaters within Cleveland. In short order, the Upper and Lower Mall Theaters became part of the Loew's Ohio Theater group, and he opened the Euclid Avenue Theater and Loew's Stillman movie theaters. Joseph Laronge was still thinking bigger and envisioned a concentration of theaters in a centralized part of Cleveland, not unlike the collection of theaters in New York City.

Left: Jay J. Allen in 1920. MacLeans Magazine, *issue 1920 02.*

Right: Jules Allen in 1920. MacLeans Magazine, *issue 1920 02.*

As the business and commercial sections of Cleveland moved away from Public Square and up Euclid Avenue, the mansions on Euclid were being torn down. This opened up tracts of land that could now be used for development. Some of the parcels were sold outright; others were leased. Laronge was able to obtain a ninety-nine-year lease on the Dodge land along Euclid Avenue and Seventeenth Street utilizing the Euclid-17th Company. The Euclid-17th Company was headed by Marcus Loew with Joseph Laronge as vice-president. Laronge was placed in charge of the construction process that would entail two theaters and a commercial building. It was these parcels of land that became the space used to build the State and Ohio Theaters.

The Bulkley Building was conceived in 1919 by the Bulkley Building Company. The company was headed by Robert J. Bulkley, son of Charles H. Bulkley, who had built the Cleveland Theater in 1885. Robert followed his father's path and entered politics shortly after he opened a law office after graduating from Harvard in 1906. He won election to the House of Representatives in 1910 and again in 1912. He was instrumental in setting up the Federal Reserve Act of 1913. During the First World War, he served as head of the legal department of the War Industries Board.

Joseph Laronge, the "Father of Playhouse Square." It was Laronge who had the idea to create a theater district in Cleveland. *Cleveland Memory Project. Playhouse Square Archives Collection.*

The building that would eventually have Bulkley's name was at the time the largest ground space of any development on Euclid Avenue and Fourteenth Street. It would eventually consist of three areas: a commercial office space eight stories tall, a garage in the rear and a theater. The theater would become the Allen Theater.

On the corner of East Seventeenth Street and Euclid Avenue, Edward Albee was acquiring space to build a large commercial building and elaborate vaudeville theater. The commercial building above the theater was modeled after the Hippodrome Theater, which Keith Theatrical Organization already owned. The theater would be one of the grandest showplaces in the country, opening up as Keith's Palace Theater.

Everything was in place for these four magnificent theaters to be built and, in the process, make Cleveland a center of the theater world in the Midwest. One last piece of the Playhouse Square puzzle was also being put in place across Euclid Avenue and down a little way on East Fourteenth Street. Daniel Rhodes Hanna, the son of Mark Hanna, wanted to build

Robert Bulkley (*center*) at a U.S. Senate banking hearing. Bulkley erected the Bulkley Building, where the Allen Theater is located. *Harris and Ewing photo, Library of Congress.*

an office space and theater in honor of his father. The family still had an interest in the Euclid Avenue Opera House down on East Fourth Street, but with all the theater activity centering on Playhouse Square and around Cleveland (there were as many as twenty additional movie theaters being built at the time), the family believed it was time to create the legacy building in Mark Hanna's name.

Playhouse Square was now ready to emerge completed with all the pieces in place and the stage set for grand openings and an entertainment district second to none in the country.

3

ARCHITECTS, BUILDERS AND BUILDINGS

I t must have been an exciting time in Cleveland at the end of 1919 and throughout 1920. The population had grown again, making the city the fifth-largest in the nation. The commercial and business sections of downtown were expanding outward and creating a first wave of urban renewal along storied Euclid Avenue. The Cleveland Indians won the World Series. There was a great deal of new construction occurring throughout the city, and Playhouse Square had all the theater projects being built about the same time.

The companies building the new theaters brought in some of the best-known architects in the country to create deluxe show palaces. Marcus Loew and Joseph Laronge contracted with Thomas Lamb to design and build the State and Ohio Theaters. The Allen brothers brought in C. Howard Crane, fresh off the successes of building a number of Fox theaters in Detroit and other places in the country. Edward Albee hired Rapp and Rapp to bring to life the Palace Theater. Finally, Daniel Hanna commissioned Charles A. Platt to design the compact auditorium of the Hanna Theater. Each theater had unique architectural fingerprints that individually and collectively made for visual masterpieces.

The State Theater was first to open, followed closely by the Ohio Theater. The Hanna Theater opened next as a showcase for legitimate theater productions. The Allen Theater opened shortly after and was built for movies. Finally, the Palace Theater opened as the "the most perfect playhouse" and the most deluxe vaudeville theater in the country.

Loew's State Theater and Ohio Theater

The property where the State and Ohio Theaters are built was part of the development purchased and leased by Joseph Laronge on the north side of Euclid Avenue having a frontage of eighty-five feet allotted for both the State and Ohio Theater entrances. It was important to have a Euclid Avenue address because of the prestige associated with that street.

The State and Ohio Theaters were designed by Thomas Lamb. Born in Scotland and arriving in the United States at the age of twelve, Lamb graduated from Cooper Union studying architecture. After working on designs for small buildings and lofts and working as a New York building inspector, he started developing plans for theaters beginning in 1909. He was approached by William Fox that year to design the City Theater on Fourteenth Street in New York. Lamb did not know much about building and designing theaters, but Fox told him that the theater should have two balconies and an orchestra pit.

Three years later, Lamb was asked to build the Regent Theater in lower Harlem by H.N. Marvin. The Regent was designed as a proper theater. It had a stage, opera boxes and a balcony with good sight lines. Although the Regent was planned for movies, Lamb's careful design touches made his name, and by 1912, he was almost exclusively designing theaters. Within a few short years, he had built and designed nine theaters in New York, more than any other architect. The theaters associated with Lamb included some of the most famous showhouses in the city—the Strand (1914), the Rialto (1916), the Rivoli (1917) and the Capitol (1918).

At the time he was contracted to build the State and Ohio Theaters in Cleveland, he had worked on more than three hundred theaters and was one of the most famous theater architects in the world. His primary design mode followed the Adams style. The style dated back to the eighteenth century and was one of the first that integrated architectural style with interiors in a uniform scheme. It was neoclassical at its heart, and Lamb believed that this style appealed to Americans. However, the State Theater may have been one of his earliest departures from following a strict Adams school. The decorations and furnishings closely followed an Italian Renaissance Middle period.

As such, the State Theater was designed as Italian Renaissance with integrated Roman, Greek and European baroque designs. These design features had coiffured ceilings and marble fireplace mantels still visible today. The ceiling relief patterns show garlands, erotes, cupids and cornucopia indicative of the Adams style. Also part of the stylistic interior designs were Greek symbols connected to Dionysus, a symbol of prosperity and drama in Greek art that was found in many grandly designed theaters of this time. Lamb made ample use of those designs throughout the lobby and auditorium.

The eighty-five-foot frontage restrictions presented an interesting design problem for the two theaters. The State Theater would have a main auditorium and stage area built behind the space being used for Keith's theater. The Ohio Theater would be built next to the State. The result was the creation of two long theater lobbies.

The State Theater lobby ended up being three continuous foyers measuring 320 feet long and 47 feet wide. The length made for

Thomas Lamb, the architect who designed Cleveland's State and Ohio Theaters. *From* National Vaudeville Artist, *1926.*

the longest lobby serving one auditorium in the country. The floor was Vermont marble and terrazzo. At the time, the *Cleveland Plain Dealer* noted that "it is possible to afford accommodations to waiting patrons in greater numbers than the theater itself."

Thomas Lamb's company and Marcus Loew employed one of the few women in the country working as a theater architect. Anne H. Dornin was born in Norfolk, Virginia, and was one of the first women to graduate from Columbia University School of Architecture. According to Dornin, "the schooling was not as difficult as the problem of finding a position of any description…. [She] just could not convince them that a woman would take the work seriously."

It was Lamb who provided the first real architectural job for her when she was asked to work with Lamb on Loew's Metropolitan Theater in Brooklyn, New York. At the time, it was the largest photoplay theater in America. Based on her work on that job and other theaters being overseen by Lamb, she was placed in charge of theater decor for Loew's Incorporated. While working for Loew's, she developed the "Theatre Decorators' Color Chart." The chart had certain criteria used to determine what colors would be used inside a theater.

The guidelines from the color chart can be seen in the color designs of the State Theater. The basic color scheme of gold and ivory with red carpets and draperies trimmed in gold follow the suggestions Dornin presented in her Decorators' Color Chart.

Anne was the on-site supervisor for Lamb and Loew. She was involved in every aspect of the construction trades while the theater was being built. Working directly with foremen on the orchestra pit, interior design and aisle dimensions and with plasterers, she had a great deal of influence. Much of her decorator tastes show up in the State Theater's final look.

The outer lobby of the State Theater originally housed a freestanding ticket booth. The floor was of white Vermont marble. The second part of the lobby continued the Vermont marble flooring with the addition of a terrazzo finish. The polished terrazzo provided both beauty and stability over time for a floor that would be walked on often.

The main lobby is dominated by four large murals along much of the length of the inner lobby. Also prominent in this section of the lobby are eight large walnut columns and two marble staircases that lead up to the balcony area. However, clearly, the focal point of the lobby is James Daugherty's murals.

James Daugherty, born in Asheville, North Carolina, grew up in Indiana and Ohio. He studied art in Washington, D.C., at the Pennsylvania Academy of Fine Arts in Philadelphia and at the London School of Art in London, England. Early in his career he experimented with applying modernist color principles. These principles were the same being played with by Matisse and Delaunay. Daugherty was one of the first Americans to paint using the abstract and near-abstract compositional style. He continued to use the power of color relationships to add interest to his abstract paintings.

Starting in 1920, he began working on murals. His role as a muralist grew with time and, by the 1930s, he was one of the most famous of the New Deal muralists. The four murals painted in the lobby of the State Theater are grand and large scale, depicting American themes and heroic images. The murals are excellent representations of the command he had of formal organization and strong color sense.

The auditorium was carpeted with lush Italian red carpet designed to harmonize with the draperies. Main draperies were also red but trimmed with gold. "Two special draperies on the side walls were of black and gold with only the valances in red." The seats in the orchestra and balcony had red seat backs, but the tilted seat was a "handsome" dull gray leather. The auditorium itself was 125 feet wide and at a depth of 156

James Daugherty working on State Theater murals. *Cleveland Memory Project. Cleveland State University.*

feet. Total capacity for the theater was listed as four thousand when it opened in February 1921. There were five aisles, and it was listed that there were forty-five exits, most of which had separate fire escapes, thereby "eliminating the possibility of crowding in the event it was necessary to empty the auditorium quickly."

The sounding board had a large mural painting representing *The Gods on Mount Parnassus*, called at the time an "extremely artistic bit of work." The mural sits between another pair of marble staircases leading up to the mezzanine lounge area and on to the balcony still higher up.

The stage of the State was thirty-five feet deep and one hundred feet wide and at the time was capable of presenting the largest vaudeville and legitimate shows. A radiator screen was installed and could be put in place quickly between vaudeville acts and movie reels, depending on what the performance call sheet required.

Construction of the theater had to overcome a tricky water condition in the lower levels of the foundation. Finding a suitable ground foundation required digging at least twenty-three feet below grade, encountering a "water bearing" sand level at seventeen feet. The lower levels of the theater ended up being submerged by six feet of water. The water had to be continuously pumped out. The base of the foundation would have to be expanded another two feet around to create a cofferdam, and pumps were installed to keep the water level below the basement floor. Other buildings were under construction at the same time, and the delay and expense would end up being cost prohibitive. An alternative was to waterproof the walls from inside the basement. A specialized Cleveland contractor and engineering firm were hired to create the waterproof membrane, allowing the basement to be finished.

The other theater simultaneously being built was the Loew's Ohio Theater. Lamb was the architect in charge of this building as well and was asked to convert a section of potentially wasted space into a theater. Designed as a legitimate showhouse, it was to be the smaller of the two theaters. This smaller house was already being advertised as a leased theater to the Erlanger and Klaw theatrical group. The Ohio shared the same eighty-five-foot frontage on Euclid as the State, and the entrance again necessitated the construction of a long lobby leading to the auditorium. In fact, the Ohio had the largest lobby of any dramatic theater in the world, second only in length to the State's lobby next door.

The lobby was divided into two sections. The first was eighty feet long with a low ceiling with a blue finish and a tiled floor. Display stands were

State Lobby shortly after opening in 1921. *Cleveland Memory Project. Cleveland State University.*

placed in this section of the lobby, along with the box office. Glass doors separated this part of the lobby from the grand foyer and main lobby area.

The main lobby was truly grand and a showplace in and of itself. Lamb again used an Italian Renaissance theme, and Greek, Roman and Renaissance reliefs were prominent throughout. This part of the entrance extends back two hundred feet and narrows as patrons move to the rear entrance into the auditorium. Antique furniture was along the lobby, leading to twin staircases up to the mezzanine lounge area.

Three large murals dominated the grand lobby. The paintings were reported to be the work of Sampitrotti, a promotional ruse used to enhance the artistic value of the murals. The three murals showed the *Birth of Venus*, the *Triumph of Venus* and her consecration at the *Altar of Love*. Additionally, a large painting of the treatment of young Bacchus was at the end of the lobby between the twin staircases. The Bacchus painting was purchased at an auction sale of the effects of Count Thornet de la Trunieliere by C.A. Selzer.

Ohio Theater Lobby in 1921. *Cleveland Memory Project. Cleveland State University.*

Selzer was antiques dealer who was born in Cleveland in 1855. He started his art business in 1881, and his original store was near Public Square. As his collection grew he moved to the Hickok Building at East Ninth and Euclid Avenue. In 1918, he again relocated, to 1501 Euclid Avenue, into a building that originally housed the Cleveland Athletic Club. Shortly after he moved to this location, the Bulkley Building Company bought the space on Euclid Avenue in front of Selzer's building.

Selzer was known to travel between the United States and Europe to purchase paintings, furniture, glassware and pottery for his many clients in Ohio. Glass wares produced for Selzer were of very high quality and were found to have a customized stamping, indicating that the piece was produced and distributed by Selzer. At the time of the construction of the Ohio Theater and Bulkley Building, Selzer would "loan" articles for display at various locations on a museum plan.

The grand foyer of the Ohio was carpeted throughout with a red woven carpet supervised by the Sterling and Welch Company of Cleveland. The mezzanine lobby and lounge carried through with the same color scheme as the grand foyer. Antique gold furniture and wall hangings were placed throughout, as well. Two reproductions of paintings, also supplied by Selzer, were on either side of the entrance lobby wall.

The auditorium was decorated in soft green and ivories. Again, two murals flanked the main theater depicting pastoral scenes. Green carpeting was used throughout the hall, and eight boxes on two levels were in green with gold accents. A large crystal chandelier supplied by Selzer was placed in the center of the auditorium.

The auditorium was slated to seat fourteen hundred patrons and had a projection room. The stage dimensions were set at forty by eighty feet. Dressing rooms were touted as among the best and most modern. Plans for the addition of a pipe organ were in the works.

With the opening of the Ohio Theater, the *Cleveland Plain Dealer* boasted that the city assumed its rightful position in the theatrical world. Joseph Laronge's Ohio Theater was considered one of the best in the country devoted to legitimate theatrical entertainment. The State Theater opened on February 5, 1921, and the Ohio Theater had its first performance on February 14, 1921.

HANNA THEATER

In April 1919, Danial Rhodes Hanna, son of Mark Hanna, began construction of a tribute to his late father. Daniel Hanna, born in 1866, followed his father into the mining and shipping businesses, becoming a member of the M.A. Hanna Company. He also tried his hand in the newspaper business, as did his father, buying the *Cleveland News* and the *Sunday News-Leader* in 1910. In Cleveland's competitive news industry, Hanna worked hard and invested to make the circulation of the papers increase. As part of his investment, in 1912, he built a new headquarters for the *News-Leader*, a fourteen-story masterpiece on Superior Avenue and East Sixth Street. It was in constructing the Leader Building that Hanna worked with Charles A. Platt, the architect of the Hanna Building and Hanna Annex. Despite Hanna's best efforts, he lost the circulation war and *Cleveland News* was bought out by the *Cleveland Plain Dealer*.

Charles Platt was a New York architect who originally trained as a landscape painter. He attended the National Academy of Design and the Académie Julian in Paris. In 1900, he received a bronze medal at the

View of completed Hanna Building in 1923. *Cleveland Memory Project. Cleveland State University.*

Paris Exposition Universelle. Platt turned to architecture shortly after that, designing mansions throughout Upstate New York and New York City. In 1907, Platt designed the Sara Delano Roosevelt townhouse on East Sixty-Fifth Street in New York City (a National Historic Landmark).

The Hanna Building was erected on land where the Euclid Avenue Presbyterian Church had existed on the corner of East Fourteenth Street and Euclid Avenue. The sixteen-story building and the eight-story annex occupy frontage on both Euclid and East Fourteenth. The main building was set at a slight angle on the corner of Euclid and East Fourteenth, and both buildings had a classical Indiana limestone exterior. As early as 1921, the *Cleveland Plain Dealer* called the building "the first gate to Playhouse Square." The paper also called the building a place of wonder for Clevelanders, with stores for the passing public and a spacious entrance leading to a circular corridor leading to another entrance on East Fourteenth Street. The decorations and interior blends with the colors of green, red, yellow and blue had a distinctly Pompeian motif. The upper floors were designed for business, and many respected firms in the city planned to set up offices at the Hanna.

Nestled on East Fourteenth Street in the Hanna Annex is the Hanna Theater. Unlike the other theaters opening at Playhouse Square, this one seemed less ostentatious. However, the theater was not simple or less spectacular than the cross-street neighbors, and to say so would be a great understatement. The lobby presents itself more like a New York theater. It is compact and direct as guests enter from Fourteenth Street, and the classic details of Italian Renaissance and Pompeian decorations are quickly apparent.

The box office lobby was gray limestone with gold cornices leading to paneled glass doors allowing entrance to the foyer. Just inside the main lobby, two curving staircases led to either side of the balcony. Soundproof doors connected the foyer and the auditorium. Travertine, a straw-colored stone from the Tiber, is used throughout the auditorium, contrasting the multicolored dome and walls that continue the Pompeian theme.

The Hanna Theater truly shines in the auditorium. Faustino Sampietro, a painter and muralist from New York, had control of the main orchestra-area decorations. His work began with dark green seats with leather bottoms surrounded by green-and-gold carpeting.

On the left side of the orchestra seating area was a lounge. The walls were frescoed, and the room had parquet floors and Louis XVI furniture. A refreshment bar was placed within the lounge, even though the 1920s was a

Hanna Theater ceiling, showing literature's great writers, placed over the proscenium. *Author's photo, 2017.*

dry era. The orchestra seating area had 827 seats, and the twenty-four rows were spaced thirty-one inches apart. Daniel Hanna was over six feet tall, and he wanted the rows to provide ample room for patrons—more than the twenty-six inches suggested by building codes. Hanna wanted even more room for his chosen seat area, row five, and the difference between rows four and five was thirty-five inches.

The Hanna Theater had one upper seating area, but just below the mezzanine were two boxes on the right and left sides of the house. The mezzanine had four rows, and above those seats were ten rows of balcony. The upper seating could hold 570 guests, bringing the total capacity to 1,421, including the 24 box seats. The patrons in the upper seating area were privileged to have front-row seats to the Sampietro coiffered ceiling.

The ceiling had multiple rows of circular and octagonal medallions alternating between each type. Each of the medallions was separated by gilded borders. Within the medallions were dragons, cupids, Psyche and merhorses immersed in a deep greenish-blue background. On the arch above the proscenium, guests could see the names of ancient and historical writers: Aeschylus, Sheridan, Euripides, Moliére, Goethe, Shakespeare and Hugo. The names were engraved across the whole of the ceiling above the stage front. The ceiling was worth the price of admission from the balcony seating area.

The proscenium was thirty-six feet, and the stage itself was forty feet by forty-two feet. Complete with counterweights and a switchboard, the scenery could be changed quickly. Stage lighting was complemented by five lights across the stage proper.

Lighting in the auditorium was dominated by four large chandeliers spread out across the theater. Each was wired for electricity, and the light shone both on the patrons below and the ceiling above.

At stage level there were two dressing suites and two large dressing rooms one level above. Up a flight of stairs on the third and fourth levels were five dressing areas. The star's dressing area, on the main floor, had a tub and shower with hot and cold running water. There was also a reception area in the front of the main dressing suite. Three more dressing rooms could be found in the basement level set up for the chorus.

Platt provided an orchestra pit and space for musicians to gather. He also planned for space to store property and costumes. Finally, under the stage area was space for electricians to both store equipment and have a storage or an office area.

The *Plain Dealer* headlines on opening night called the memorial to Senator Hanna one of the "nation's finest temples of drama." Though Pompeii is long gone, the Pompeian color scheme and decorations provide a peek into what might have been the appearance of an ancient city prior to the rage of Mount Vesuvius. A fitting memorial to Daniel Hanna's father and an outstanding addition to Cleveland's theater scene, the Hanna Theater opened on March 28, 1921.

ALLEN THEATER AND BULKLEY BUILDING

The Allen Theater was a part of the planning for the Bulkley Building from the beginning. The estimated cost of the building ran about $4 million. The building was planned to have a frontage of two hundred feet on the north side of Euclid and a footprint of two acres. The land was held under a ninety-nine-year lease and would consist of an eight-story office building (more than two hundred offices), commercial space on the ground floor and the theater. Two entrance lobbies were part of the design. One entrance lobby would serve only as an access to the Allen Theater. The second entrance

Bulkley Building during construction. Seen here is the showroom of C. Selzer, who contributed artwork on loan to the new theaters. *Cleveland Memory Project. Cleveland State University.*

would act as the lobby to the main building, creating an arcade with several additional stores.

The Bulkley was also designed with a garage in the basement that would extend underneath the theater. The garage size was planned for 120 cars and covers the rear of the building. The front part of the basement was to be leased to the Colonnade Company for a high-grade restaurant.

The jewel of the new building was the planned Allen Theater, to be run by Jules and Jay Allen. In 1920, the Allen brothers operated the largest chain of theaters in Canada. They were looking to expand in the United States, and they chose Detroit and Cleveland.

The Allens hired C. Howard Crane to design and build the new theater space within the Bulkley Building. Born in 1885 in Connecticut, Crane began his architectural career in Detroit at the turn of the century with no formal training. His early works were mainly bank and office buildings. He moved on to build grand theaters; most were referred to as movie palaces. None of the large theaters he built had capacities under twenty-five hundred patrons. His designs were elaborate, with craftsmanship that paid great attention to detail. Since many of the theaters he built would hold musical performances associated with the movies, his theaters generally had wonderful acoustics. Crane built more than 250 movie theaters throughout the country and in Britain. His most famous was the Fox Theater in Detroit, but he also designed Olympia Stadium, where the Detroit Red Wings played, the Lafayette Building in Detroit and the Leveque Tower in Columbus, Ohio.

Crane's penchant for deluxe movie theaters continued with his designs for the Allens. Patrons entering the Allen Theater crossed a 133-foot lobby entrance that had a slight incline leading from the ticket kiosk just outside the main doors. The lobby wall was mirrored with a coiffured ceiling following the Italian Renaissance theme Crane selected for the theater.

Guests found a rotunda modeled after the Villa Madonna, located just outside of Rome, at the end of the lobby. The *Plain Dealer* stated, "It will be without question the most discussed portion of the new house." The rotunda was thirty-three feet high and had great mahogany columns supporting the dome. In the center of the marble floor was a fountain, and above the fountain was suspended a large chandelier in the center of the dome. The mezzanine balcony overlooked the floor of the rotunda with excellent sight lines. Clearly, Crane's design was meant to impress—and the goal was achieved.

Additionally, Crane's original design drawings set out two rooms on either side of the rotunda. On the right was a tearoom meant to provide opportunities for patrons to relax with a light bite to eat while awaiting the next movie showing or before or after the performance. On the left was the men's lounge, where gentlemen could sit and relax as well as view the movie.

Just past the rotunda on the other side of the columns and through heavy curtains, patrons entered the main floor of the auditorium. The Italian Renaissance theme and color scheme continued into the seating area. Deep-red furnishings were found throughout the auditorium area. On either side of the viewing hall were large faux windows that concealed lights that coordinated a range of color hues against the walls.

The auditorium sloped down toward an orchestra pit area in front of the stage. The stage itself was large enough not only for the movie screen but also to allow for other presentations such as prologue or epilogue events or concerts if desired.

The balcony and mezzanine area allowed for good sight lines of the presentations. The projection booth was in the rear of the balcony, allowing for an excellent angle of dispersion for "throwing" the film onto the screen. The balcony and mezzanine had a promenade area, and patrons could view below the upper seating area to the main floor seating.

Overall, the Allens and Crane created a "fairyland" scene seating three thousand moviegoers in luxury. The theater was supplied and operated by the most advanced movie equipment and operators and was considered one of the premier deluxe movie houses in the country. It opened on April 1, 1921, to great fanfare and expectations.

B.F. Keith Palace Theater

In an interview with the *Plain Dealer* about the time the Palace Theater opened, Edward Albee said, "I was impressed with two attributes of the city, it was a city of home folks...who took pride in their dwellings and in owning them and that its interests were diversified." Those simple tenets convinced him that Cleveland should be the home for the most magnificent playhouse in the Keith Circuit.

Keith Vaudeville was in Cleveland starting with the company's purchase of the Prospect Theater in 1904 and the expansion purchase of the Hippodrome Theater in 1908. Although vaudeville was the most popular form of entertainment in the country, Keith's business had a difficult time establishing a foothold in the city. The massive Hippodrome did not make a profit until 1918. And in 1918, A. Paul Keith died from the Spanish flu. Albee, who for all practical purposes was the head of the Keith Entertainment Company and the Vaudeville Circuit, became the sole owner and head of the circuit and all of its properties.

Albee began in earnest to survey the city and find a desirable location of a new vaudeville house. He settled on the corner of Euclid Avenue and East Seventeenth Street. This corner was once the homestead of the Samuel Dodge family, one of the first families in the city, in 1798. It was also the eastern end of the land being cobbled together by Joseph Laronge to create a center for theatrical performances.

C.W. and George Rapp were contracted to be the architects for the Palace Theater. The Rapp brothers, both born in Carbondale, Illinois, are part of a unique family. The Rapps are the only family in history to have produced four famous architects in one generation followed by three in the next. The Rapp and Rapp architecture firm placed a single idea at the top of every theater it built: eye-popping opulence.

The opulence begins as soon as guests enter the outer lobby. Imported marble from Carrara, Italy, greets patrons as they enter off Euclid Avenue. The spiderweb and butterfly mirror images in the marble immediately find your eye. Beauty is balanced with convenience in the first part of the spacious lobby, with two ticket offices on either side. The box offices were made of bronze and provided space for employees to greet guests and provide entrance tickets for multiple performances.

As one entered the theater's Grand Hall through a set of bronze doors, "the increasing beauty of the theater development becomes marked." The spiderweb effect in the marble continued atop two sweeping staircases, also made of marble. The Grand Hall was exquisitely lit by five imported Czechoslovakian crystal chandeliers. As visitors' eyes darted around the hall, their feet were cushioned by a large, one-piece woven carpet, also imported from Czechoslovakia. The carpet was the largest single-piece woven carpet in the world and was shipped to Cleveland on two flatcars.

The Grand Hall of the B.F. Keith Palace Theater in Cleveland, Ohio, in 1922. *From Playhouse Square Tour Guide Manual PL 26.*

The walls abound with artistic masterpieces placed throughout the great hall and displayed in panels built specifically for the walls in the Palace. The artwork found in the Grand Hall and Promenade were all selected by Albee, and many were from his personal collection. The paintings include *Le Chef Arabe* by Adolf Schreyer, a German painter of the Dusseldorf school, and *The Shoal Fisher* by Jozef Israels, a Dutch master who was among the most respected Dutch artists of the second half of the nineteenth century. *The Shoal Fisher* was sold by Sotheby's in 2005 for $335,000. There were pastorals and portraits from French masters and marble sculptures, some of which came from the J.P. Morgan collection. Rare tapestries, bronzes, a rare blue urn porcelain piece (purchased from C.A. Selzer) and textiles were set throughout the Grand Hall, Promenade and the small rooms surrounding each. Louis XVI furniture and antique tables were set about the hall and sitting rooms. Albee's eye for detail made the lobby of the Palace Theater a downtown art gallery.

Edward Jonas, president of the Chamber Syndicate of Fine Arts in France, was quoted as saying, "Paris had nothing like this, nor London, Vienna or Rome." He also stated that "it will be surprising if Cleveland is a long time wakening to the art value of the Keith Theater." The art and treasures in the lobbies presented a fear that patrons would prefer to linger viewing the artwork to entering the auditorium for the performance.

Should any Clevelander linger in the lobbies and forget to enter the auditorium, they would have seen only part of the splendor of the Palace. Entering the main performance area through four arched doors, guests entered an auditorium that contained no pillars and allowed excellent views of the stage. Marble walls continued in the main seating area, and the large panels of marble were filled with additional painting masterpieces. Silk brocade wall hangings were along the side walls.

The crystal lighting used to illuminate the Grand Hall continued to be a theme throughout the auditorium. Crystal fixtures were placed everywhere in the main seating area. Guests walked under the balcony area, where the lighting fixtures were distributed around the ceiling, allowing patrons to easily find their seats. The ivory-and-gold color scheme exuded the richness sought by Albee and his architects.

Once out from under the balcony cover, visitors could look up and take in the exquisite molded plaster ceiling. The conventional figures carefully created by the sculptor's hand enhanced the Imperial French style sought within and throughout the theater. The 3,680 seats were arranged in a tiered manner on a solid reinforced concrete floor. Heavy carpeting placed in the aisles was rich and comfortable.

The upper seating area had wraparound box seats, a mezzanine area and an upper balcony seating space. At the top of the balcony, skyboxes provided an expansive view of the entire auditorium. The balcony was and is an architectural wonder, as Rapp and Rapp was one of the architectural firms that refined and perfected the cantilever balcony construction process starting in the early 1900s. The design process allowed for the use of a rigid beam anchored on only one side, eliminating external support columns. The elimination of columns provided audiences with clear views of the entire stage area.

The stage of the Palace Theater was considered large at fifty-nine feet wide and ninety feet deep. The proscenium was thirty-five feet high; on either side of the stage, two seven-story towers contained dressing areas and performers' amenities.

The dressing areas were the finest in the country. The lower-level rooms contained marble baths and showers, while the upper-level rooms had access to restroom facilities on each floor. The ivory-and-gold color pattern found in the auditorium and lobby areas was included in the performers' rooms. The dressing rooms followed a pattern established in Keith theaters by Harry Jordon, a manager in Philadelphia. At the Chestnut Street Theater, Jordon was looking for a way to reduce arguments between performers regarding the assignment of dressing areas. Rather than label a dressing area as "star," he determined that all dressing rooms would be named after a state. This reduced disagreements between performers and soothed egos during their run at the theater.

All dressing areas were provided with a chest of drawers, dressing tables and mirrors. Ice water for drinking was available. The conveniences were not limited to the headline performers. Special retiring rooms and restrooms existed for the chorus girls at the upper levels of the dressing tower.

On the opposite side of the stage area, the amenities included a beauty parlor, a tailor shop, a laundry room, a barbershop, a billiards room and a miniature-golf course. The theater provided space for animals to rest and run, including a grooming area to keep those performers looking good.

Performers traveled as families and, following the Keith Circuit, might remain in a city for a week to ten days or longer. Many performers had family acts, and with the two-a-day and continuous performance schedules, the family had to remain at the theater for most of the day. The Palace Theater provided a children's nursery and play area for the younger members of the performers' families.

The elegance was recognized by performers as soon as they entered the theater. The entrance to the stage door looked like the lobby of a fine

Backstage nursery provided to vaudeville families while performing at the Keith's Palace Theater. *Cleveland Memory Project. Cleveland State University.*

hotel. Actors would register at a counter, where security would keep an eye on the stage door, pick up the keys to their dressing rooms and check for mail. The first-class treatment was appreciated by the actors, actresses and their families. There was even a kitchen area on the top floor of the west section back stage with all the equipment needed to make a quick meal.

Members of the orchestra also had retiring rooms and access to bathrooms. There was a musical library and a gathering area. These amenities were located in the lower levels of the theater and shared space with the same retiring areas provided to stage employees and even charwomen.

Outside of the auditorium were amenities galore for the patrons. A ground-floor women's room with an artistically finished plaster ceiling served as a refuge from the performance before, during and after the show. The room had a large fireplace mantel acquired by Albee out of an old home with a large sectional mirror over it. Another room decorated in an Egyptian motif served as a smoking area for women. The men's rest area had the look of a formal private club. This area had a large table, comfortable chairs and private telephone booths. It was cast in dark wood, found in the finest of private clubs.

Even the house manager had accommodations that were first class. A suite of three rooms equipped with its own bath was located off the Grand Hall along the Promenade. It was here that the manager of the Palace would conduct business, and the area provided space for the productions' managers to work and schedule shows.

All in all, the Keith Palace Theater was designed and built by Albee to act as the pinnacle of the Keith Entertainment Circuit. It was constructed to honor the late B.F. Keith by his partner and business associate, and it was to be the "world's finest theater."

4

OPENING NIGHTS

T he planning and vision of Joseph Laronge and Loew's Ohio Theater group, the newest of Loew's Theatrical Corporation theaters and the first installment of what was hoped to be a large expansion in the United States by the Allen Brothers and the memorial built to remember his father by Daniel Rhodes Hanna, all came to reality between February and April 1921. The celebration of performances honoring the builders and investors in a great city created a civic and cultural excitement rarely seen in Cleveland—or any city, for that matter. The marvelous and deluxe showplaces were about to make their graduation walk to the public at large after the who's who festivity of the opening nights.

The wonderment began with elaborate ceremonies put on by Marcus Loew to introduce Cleveland to Loew's State Theater. The three-day celebration started with the arrival at 10:00 a.m. of two specially chartered train cars at Union Station. Marcus Loew was present, and his entourage was met by a reception of nearly one hundred people representing the Al Sirat Grotto No. 17, the Rotary Club of Cleveland and the Kiwanis Clubs of Cleveland. Traveling with Mr. Loew were cameramen from Metro Studios and upward of thirty movie stars. At the time, it was estimated that the photoplay stars attending would be the largest ever assembled for the opening of a new film theater.

The large number of movie stars attending was in part due to the fact that Marcus Loew had purchased the Metro Movie production company in 1920 to help feed the theater chain's need for entertainment. It was his first foray into the production of movies, but not his last. Over the next several years, Loew's Entertainment would buy Mayor Production and Golden movie production companies and stitch together the movie conglomerate MGM. At first, Metro Movies and then later MGM would be exclusively shown within the Loew's Theater group.

An automobile parade led by mounted police and the eighty-five-piece Grotto Band brought the stars and dignitaries to city hall. Mayor William FitzGerald provided a key to the city, and the parade continued on to Public Square. Lunch was served at the Statler Hotel as part of the weekly Rotary meeting. The festivities continued with a tour of the outlying city areas and more food at the Clifton Club. Sites visited around the city included Rockefeller Park, Lake Shore Boulevard, Shaker Lakes and Edgewater Park.

At seven o'clock, the doors to the State Theater opened, allowing guests and dignitaries an hour before opening ceremonies to roam the new theater and take in the spectacular sights. The governor of the State of Ohio, Cleveland's mayor, Mr. Loew and many of the assembled stars took turns speaking during the ceremonies. After the opening speeches, Hyman L. Spitalny presented a musical overture that included *Finlandia* by Sibelius and a violin trio presentation performed by Spitalny himself. The movie *Polly with a Past* starring Ina Claire was the feature, surrounded by a comedy and short reel subjects.

The stars and celebrities remained in Cleveland throughout the weekend and into Monday. They visited the many Loew's Theaters around town (Stillman, Euclid, Alhambra, Mall, Park and Liberty) and attended return engagements to greet guests at the State Theater. The *Plain Dealer* had an entire section devoted to the opening and the surrounding events.

The day after the opening, besides continued visits by stars and celebrities, female guests attending the performance that day could attend a tea service on the mezzanine level of the State Theater. The tea service was part of a custom Loew had started in Boston. Women could expect to have tea served every afternoon between 2:00 and 4:00 p.m.

Overall, Marcus Loew set a very high bar for openings, and the city of Cleveland opened its doors wide to start the celebrations for the new series of theaters at Playhouse Square. It was a start that was difficult to re-create. Next up was Loew's Ohio Theater's new dramatic showcase next door to the State.

After all the celebration, parades and visits by celebrities at the State Theater, opening night for the Ohio Theater was more muted. The headlines were not about stars' visitations, except for one star. The newspapers took time to review the new house for its beauty and the beauty of the foyer. The *Plain Dealer* also described the experience guests would have as they came to the Ohio auditorium through the longest lobby in the world for a dramatic playhouse. The visual sights of C.A. Selzer's paintings and antiques in the lobby as well as the experience of being called to the auditorium at the start of the performance and at the end of intermission by four Italian bells was surely a pleasant experience. The interior design and color selection by Phillip Garbo found praise by the first-nighters. The real news, however, was about David Warfield's performance and David Belasco, the producer of the play *The Return of Peter Grimm.*

On a crisp thirty-degree evening, February 14, 1921, patrons filed into the Ohio Theater to see the second opening of Cleveland's new Playhouse Square theaters. The Ohio presented an interesting play staring David Warfield and produced by David Belasco. The storyline is about Peter Grimm, a patriarch who ruled his family like a monarch. After arranging for the marriage of his ward to his nephew, Grimm dies. The story within a story then proceeds as Grimm returns in a ghostly form neither seen nor heard by the other players and attempts to have his wishes fulfilled. Warfield, in the title role, presents what was described by one critic as "the greatest exhibition of acting ever witnessed." The play was a revival for Belasco of the hit he had presented on Broadway. It was a resounding success in Cleveland. It was also an interesting foreshadowing of the future of the Ohio Theater.

While Clevelanders waited for the next opening, the State and Ohio Theaters captured the bulk of the interest and theatergoing public over the next several weeks. After *Polly with a Past*, the State Theater featured a Douglas Fairbanks movie (*The Mark of Zorro*) and a Mary Pickford movie (*Love Light*), as well as the film *Always Audacious*. According to one published report, the State Theater hosted eighteen thousand guests in one day. At the Ohio, a George Cohan production, *The Acquittal*, starring William Harrigan and the entire New York original cast, followed *Peter Grimm*. Helen Hayes, the eighteen-year-old starlet performer, was next up in *Bab* and performed to rave reviews.

A few weeks later, the Hanna Theater opened its doors for the first time. The Hanna would pose competition to the Ohio and presumably take up and continue the mantle of the Euclid Avenue Opera House. On March 28, 1921, the memorial to Mark Hanna by his son Daniel opened for guests on another cold evening. Cleveland's well-heeled crowded into the small lobby and past the box office to see the impressive work of Charles Platt and Faustino Sampietro for the first time. The house was oversold, as more than fifteen hundred patrons crowded about the new theater. Many of the guests were regular ticket holders to the venerable opera house previously linked to the Hanna family.

The new dramatic house opened with an adaptation of Mark Twain's *The Prince and the Pauper*. William Faversham, who was well known to Cleveland audiences, played the part of Miles Hendon, a man who helps restore the prince to his rightful place. Ruth Findlay had the dual lead role and was well received. The orchestra director was Max Faetkenheuer, who opened the evening with "The Star-Spangled Banner" and an overture of Mozart's *Le nozze di Figaro*.

It was the general consensus, in the words of one critic, that there had never been a theater "so perfectly adapted to drama." The *Plain Dealer* seconded the description, calling the Hanna Theater one of the finest dramatic houses in all the country.

As exciting as the opening of the Hanna was, Cleveland could neither rest nor celebrate for long. Three days later, the Allen Theater held a grand opening. The Allen was one of two film-only theater houses opened by the Allen Brothers in Cleveland. The Canadian movie-theater owners would also open the Capital Theater at Gordon Square a week later. The Allen on Euclid Avenue in the new Bulkley Building was the flagship of their venture into the United States.

Thousands traveled to Euclid Avenue to be at the opening of the new theater at Playhouse Square. As patrons walked into the mirrored lobby, they immediately entered a fairyland. Chandeliers and concealed wall lights illuminated the walk-through, allowing the mirrors to reflect and expand the atmosphere.

Once past the gently sloped lobby, Clevelanders arrived at the rotunda encircled by lofty columns two stories tall. The dome of the rotunda contained another chandelier that again bounced light throughout the entrance walkway. In the middle of the scene was a fountain placed directly below the chandelier. A refreshment room—a tearoom—was to one side of the marvelous domed entrance. Many of Cleveland's best started their night with an informal dinner in the tearoom prior to the start of the formal program.

Past the curtains and up in the balcony and mezzanine area, the light show did not end. Numerous various-colored lights created a surreal atmosphere. The concealed globes reflected light throughout the auditorium, providing multicolor hues gracing the faux windows on either side of the seating area. More light was sent out from the stage area, and all the lights blended perfectly with the deep-red furnishings.

As patrons settled into their seats and looked in amazement at this newest deluxe photoplay house, Bruce Metcalfe played the first chords on the Kimball pipe organ. The music from this grand organ began at 8:00 p.m. Cleveland was about to inaugurate the fourth Playhouse Square theater.

The feature shown that evening was *The Greatest Passion* starring Vera Gordon. But before the program began, Phil Spitalny, brother of Hyman Spitalny, called his thirty-five orchestra members to attention and played "The Star-Spangled Banner." The audience rose in unison, and the program started in earnest. The overture was Tchaikovsky's *Capriccio Italien*, in keeping with the general architectural surroundings of the Allen. The program proceeded with a news reel, an educational and a scenic film and the musical prologue to the feature film, and it ended with a comedy, *High and Dry*.

The evening was not done for Cleveland's first-nighters when the show ended. The honored guests that evening included the Allen brothers, Mr. and Mrs. Bulkley, officials from the Allen syndicate and guests from Toronto, Chicago and Detroit (C. Howard Crane and his guests), as well as many Cleveland elected officials. Most of those in this group remained after the program and danced in the rotunda until midnight. The fourth and last opening at Playhouse Square in 1921 surely left everyone satisfied and looking foward to when the final show palace would open in 1922.

Cleveland had to wait nineteen months, but the opening of Keith's Palace Theater was another gala affair. The city's famous and near-famous waited on the evening of November 6, 1922, to see firsthand the "finest theater in the world." As crowds entered the lobby and observed the fine artwork, furniture and tapestries, they were surely amazed. Edward Albee constructed and furnished a true palace. There are many theaters around the country incorporating the word *palace*, but none were like Keith's. Opening night observers claimed that no European capital had a theater to compare to the richness and luxury of the Palace.

Albee's dream to create a lasting edifice to his business partner, B.F. Keith, was achieved magnificently. His attention to detail and personal selection of the artwork and furniture contributed to a royal and first-class playhouse for the Keith Vaudeville Circuit. The surroundings and theater itself were the true stars of the night. However, the opening night program was equal to the building itself.

Headlining the program was Elsie Janis, who performed a number of personations from a familiar repertoire. Her singing and voice impersonations were spot-on, and the mimicry was very funny. As William

McDermott from the *Plain Dealer* stated, "The audience paid her a tribute at least twice as exuberant as they paid the handsome velvet curtains." The program also showcased an Italian comic, Harry Burns; a crooner in a soldier's uniform; and a dance group, the Cansinos, which closed the show. The musicians played some wonderful jazz, and the audience remained until the end of the last chord.

As patrons exited, they were met by a waiting crowd outside at least as large as the number in the seats. The full house was greeted and exited by handsomely attired ushers. The ushers were both men and women. Cleveland's Playhouse Square was now complete, and even New York would be a bit jealous of the luxury and opulence found in the hinterlands.

5

MUSIC, MUSICIANS AND MOVIES

I n 1908, Samuel Lionel Rothafel (Rothapfel) placed a bedsheet on the wall in a spare room behind a bar in Forest City, Pennsylvania. He set up a hand-cranked projector and charged patrons five cents to see a few reels of "living pictures." "Roxy" Rothafel experimented with new ideas to keep the guests pleased, including a curtain that opened and closed to start and end a movie, colored lights to add atmosphere, a piano player augmented by a violinist and classical singers. His little theater was renting as many or more reels as the largest theaters in New York, and other owners took notice. So began the expanding entertainment of going out for the evening to see a movie.

Roxy Rothafel's success led B.F. Keith and then Marcus Loew to him to upgrade the venues of large New York City theaters. Roxy began bringing in orchestras and provided improved musical scores that accompanied the movies. Rothafel believed that music supporting a movie shouldn't be canned but customized and synchronized. A great pipe organ might be interesting to support a movie, but an orchestral score of high classical music would make an evening out. He also hired and trained ushers, who provided guests with the greatest of courtesy and strived to meet patrons' needs to create a memorable evening out.

Thus, the gold standard for deluxe movie houses was set. Local movie theaters all had musical backgrounds for the shows, but for the large showcase theaters built after 1913, orchestras and musical directors were a must. Cleveland was one of the places where musical interpretations behind the movies were used early, and the city was extremely lucky to have many talented musicians and directors. Those most recognized over time were the Spitalny brothers.

In 1906, after the assassination of a police chief in Bialystok, three days of violence and murders by Tsarist soldiers took place. The Odessa pogrom (a Russian word meaning "to wreak havoc" and describing officially mandated slaughter of Jews) was the latest in an ongoing anti-Semitic purge in Russia. It was from Odessa that the Spitalny family fled for safety to the United States.

Jacob Spitalny, a violinist, was the first music teacher for his three sons, Hyman, Philip and Maurice. Hyman and Philip were already well along in their music training, both studying at the Imperial Conservatory in Odessa, when the pogrom took place. Philip was considered a musical prodigy, having played as a child throughout the Ukraine prior to entering the conservatory. Maurice arrived with the family in the United States but traveled from America later to study in Berlin. The Spitalnys eventually settled in Cleveland.

In 1911, Philip was playing at the Grand Theater in Cleveland as part of a vaudeville bill, and by 1912, Hyman had been installed as the musical director at the Knickerbocker Theater. Hyman was already known around town as the director of a concert band. Maurice had recently returned from studying in Germany to give music lessons and begin playing classical music in local theaters as well. It wasn't long before the classically trained musicians created a following and elevated the music in Cleveland's theaters and elsewhere. All would have distinguished careers, and each in their own way become quite famous outside of Cleveland.

The brothers eventually moved into directing orchestras at various venues around town. Hyman directed at the Loew's Stillman and at the Statler Hotel. Philip was musical director at the Metropolitan (located at East Fifty-Fifth and Euclid), and Maurice (Morris) led the band at the Knickerbocker on East Eighty-Third and Euclid.

As movies took hold of the viewing public, the musical accompaniments to the shows fell into two categories. Organists and bands were given music sheets that were consistently similar and uniform for the movie, no matter where the show played. This production music made it easy to move a film from venue to venue. The other way music was played for movies was customized by musical directors. The Spitalny brothers were specialists in custom music. By the time Loew's State and the Allen were opened, Hyman and Philip had musical libraries valued at nearly $20,000. Thus, the brothers' reputations and depth of resources made them the obvious choices to lead the newly opened deluxe showcases at Playhouse Square.

In an article in the *Plain Dealer*, Philip Spitalny explained how he prepared music for a feature film: "I study every picture three times before it is shown publicly." The first time was to get the atmosphere of the movie. The second time was to plan for the subtitles and select and arrange the musical score. The final time was a dress rehearsal with the orchestra to be ready for the public. Spitalny would select a theme for each character, allowing the audience to identify the lead roles. Often, the theme might change as a character's role matured throughout the film.

At the Stillman and later at Loew's State, Hyman saw his role as not only musical director but also as movie director. It usually takes sixteen minutes to display one thousand feet of film, but that time frame may vary based on various synchronizing issues. In cases when the movie reel is faster or slower than expected, the musical director might have to adjust the score to keep the music in sync with the action on the screen. Sometimes, a dramatic scene may be slowed down to add tension. The music would have reflected that same tension.

The musical selections would sometimes be classical, sometimes popular; sometimes, the Spitalny brothers composed original music to fit the movie. Phil was especially fond of modern music. Jazz was gaining popularity, and in the early 1920s, and after the Allen Theater was built, he sponsored jazz festival evenings at Playhouse Square. This was especially true after the Allens ran into film distribution problems shortly after the theater opened.

Brother Hyman was not a fan of jazz. In an article in the *Plain Dealer*, he commented that he would never play it. It was shortly after that article appeared in 1923 that Hyman moved on from the State Theater to become orchestra director at the McVicker's Symphony Orchestra in Chicago. At that time, he started to be known as H. Leopold Spitalny and by 1934 was working at NBC Radio with the RCA Victor Orchestra.

Maurice took over directing the State Theater Orchestra after Hyman left for Chicago, having spent one year as assistant concertmaster for the new Cleveland Orchestra. Maurice remained in Cleveland until 1932, when he moved to Pittsburgh and became supervisor of music at radio station KDKA. While at the State Theater, he continued the tradition of providing custom music for silent movies and show music for performances on the stage. He wrote a number of popular songs in the 1930s, and some of them were recorded by the likes of Tommy Dorsey and Johnny Messner. He also wrote songs that were featured in movies and short cartoons.

Allen Theater Orchestra, Phil Spitalny, director. Phil was one of three Spitalny brothers who worked in the theaters in Cleveland. *Cleveland Memory Project. Cleveland State University.*

Philip remained in Cleveland until 1930, when he moved to New York and started on his quintessentially quixotic project of creating a full orchestra and chorus composed completely of women. In 1934, he accomplished the goal, and Phil Spitalny and His All-Girl Orchestra gained recognition. They played on CBS radio and toured the country. Movie deals followed, and the *Hour of Charm* successfully had a twenty-year run on radio and television. The women and Phil continued to perform until 1955. Phil was one of the most successful musical entrepreneurs from the golden age of radio. The Spitalny brothers all had distinguished musical careers that began in Cleveland making music for silent movies and supporting jazz at Playhouse Square.

6

FIRST THEATER MANAGERS

ROBERT MCLAUGHLIN—THE OHIO

In the 1920s, theater managers held a great deal of power in setting schedules, finding talent and keeping the lights out front glowing. Here again Cleveland was fortunate to have a few of the best managers in the business installed at the Ohio Theater, Keith's Palace and the Hanna Theater. Each presents a fascinating story in the history of Playhouse Square.

The Ohio Theater immediately hired Robert McLaughlin, born in Pennsylvania and raised in Fostoria, Ohio, and a graduate of Ohio State University. After college, he became an editor of the *News-Democrat* in Canton, Ohio, and worked for a time as secretary to William McKinley. McLaughlin came to Cleveland in 1905 and worked in the newspaper business at the *Plain Dealer* for five years. After that, he worked as a press agent for a number of theaters around town. He enjoyed being around the theater and jumped into management. He managed the Duchess, Metropolitan and Colonial Theaters early in his theater career.

In 1915, he wrote the play *The Eternal Magdalene*. It premiered at the Colonial Theater and went on to be shown on Broadway. McLaughlin went on to write a number of other plays, including *The Sixth Commandment, Demi Tasse, Pearl of Great Price* and *Decameron Nights.* It was *Decameron Nights* that become the first play written by an American to be produced in London, at the Royal Theater, in 1922.

His connections and success as a writer and producer made him a natural choice for the new Ohio Theater. The Ohio was a legitimate house and brought in shows under the Erlanger and Klaw theater booking agency. Abe Erlanger had connections to Cleveland, having worked with John Ellsler and later at the Euclid Avenue Opera House during the Mark Hanna ownership years. The most direct competition to the Ohio would be the Hanna Theater, as both were providing Clevelanders serious stage productions.

McLaughlin had many skills that served him well as manager of the Ohio Theater. At one time, he was a part owner of the Black Cat movie studios in Cleveland and Argus Enterprises, also a movie production company. He wrote screenplays for silent movies and continued to be involved with producing stage shows in Cleveland and New York. He helped produce movies inspired by his writings and the work of other authors.

Just prior to the opening of the Ohio Theater, McLaughlin organized and produced summer stock shows that were seen at many of the Schubert-leased theaters in the city. These included the Colonial and the Euclid Opera House. When Gus Hartz, the dean of theater managers from the Opera House, retired, McLaughlin stepped in as manager and remained in charge until the venerable theater closed its doors in 1922. He continued to write plays that were part of the summer stock programs he produced and that were shown not only in Cleveland but also in other cities around the country.

As the 1920s progressed, Broadway shows were often difficult to book. McLaughlin's New York connections with both plays and movies helped to keep the marquee of the Ohio lit and the seats filled. This was especially true as theatrical syndicates were winding down and movie production trusts were gearing up. Marcus Loew was in the process of creating MGM movie studios, consolidating Metro Movies, Goldwyn Movies and Mayer Movie studios, to continue to provide his numerous theaters with films for the viewing public. William Fox, a one-time partner with McLaughlin in the Cleveland movie production enterprise, was building a movie-studio empire and the Warner brothers were also creating an entertainment corporation. Adolph Zukor was creating Paramount Studios out of the Famous Players–Lasky movie studios.

Although the Ohio Theater was primarily a "legit" stagehouse, McLaughlin soon arranged for movies to be shown at the Ohio. In fact, in the early to mid-1920s, the Ohio Theater gave Cleveland audiences the most famous road-show silent movies of the time. These included *The Ten Commandments* (1923) and *Beau Geste* (1926), distributed by Famous-Lasky and Paramount Pictures, Adolph Zukor's company; and *Ben-Hur* (1925), distributed by MGM. McLaughlin's connections to Loew and his ties to movie production companies helped to bring these blockbuster road shows into Cleveland. It early on established the Ohio Theater as a venue that could sustain road shows. Both *The Ten Commandments* and *Ben-Hur* returned to the Ohio for long engagements when they were remade in the 1950s.

Under McLaughlin's management, the Ohio Theater premiered several Broadway blockbusters in the 1920s. These included *No, No, Nanette* and *Show Boat* prior to the Broadway openings of both productions. Late in the decade, McLaughlin was able to bring to the stage Eugene O'Neill's *Strange Interlude* (1929), a very long production that began at 5:30 p.m. with a dinner intermission.

As the decade progressed and closed, Robert McLaughlin was able to keep the lights on in the Ohio most every week. The shows continued through the summer as he continued to produce and operate a summer stock program and used the cast and shows to fill in during the regular theater season after the stock market crashed.

McLaughlin worked the Ohio Theater until the weight of the Depression forced the stage to close. He was not, however, done with Cleveland. In the early 1930s, McLaughlin took over the summer stock programs at the Hanna Theater. This development was the result of a break between ownership at the Ohio Theater and the Erlanger booking agency when Abe Erlanger passed away. A brief attempt to revive summer stock at the Ohio in 1932 lasted only part of that season. In 1934, he was hired as the manager for the Public Auditorium and Music Hall for the City of Cleveland and briefly tried to bring life back into the Ohio Theater.

He was also associated with an attempt to create the Townhall Theater at the former Higbee's building; however, the capital needed could never be raised. He finally left Cleveland and headed to Hollywood to write screenplays for the movies. Work was just as difficult in Hollywood, and his time there did not last long. He returned to Cleveland for the last months of his life.

John F. Royal—The Palace

Born in 1886 in Boston, John F. Royal started his working life as the night office boy for the *Boston Post* and moved his way up to reporter. Among his most memorable news posts was the scoop in 1905 on the peace conference in Portsmouth, New Hampshire, that ended the Russo-Japanese War. His connections in Boston led to a job in public relations with the Keith Orpheum Circuit at the age of twenty-four. Among the performers he promoted was Houdini.

The Keith organization moved him to manager of theaters in Boston and Cincinnati before he was brought to Cleveland in 1916, when he replaced longtime Keith manager of the Hippodrome Harry Daniels. Daniels was taking a break after ten years at the Hippodrome, but John Royal proved to be an important promoter and community asset, thereby remaining at the Hipp. It was while at the Hippodrome that Keith's operation at that theater finally began to make a consistent profit. Vaudeville in general and Keith's circuit in particular finally gained a strong foothold in Cleveland, and guests began filling the seats.

When Edward Albee and the Keith Theater group determined to build the "world's finest" theater in Cleveland, John Royal was the natural choice to manage the Palace Theater. He was involved with opening not only the Palace but also Keith's 105th Street Theater.

Prior to opening and managing the Palace, John Royal was a true community member. He was part of the U.S. War Bond program in Cleveland while at the Hippodrome and, during one drive, used his promotional skills combined with vaudeville acts to raise more than $264,000 for the effort. He was a member of the Cleveland Rotary Club and was praised by the *Plain Dealer* as always being generous with access to Keith Theaters during the war and afterward whenever a public gathering was being planned. Royal held Christmas parties for children and provided entertainment for VIP gatherings. He soon was considered one of the pillars of community service throughout the Cleveland area.

He had clout within the Keith Circuit. Theater managers were not only in charge of the day-to-day running of the theater but were also often responsible for putting together programs that met the requirements of the public. He traveled around the eastern United States and even to Europe in search of talent to bring into the Keith Circuit and to Cleveland. As a result of his efforts, many of the biggest stars of the 1920s and some of the up-and-coming acts came to the city to perform. Until 1925, the Palace Theater was a vaudeville house only and represented the best of what "big vaudeville" two-a-days were all about.

Between seasons, John Royal was able to fill the Palace with stellar visits by the Chicago Opera Company and various ballet companies. After 1925, the Palace presented continuous vaudeville performances supplemented with movies—film began to become the rage for most of the theatergoing public. He was a manager and promoter in the best sense of both words. He was aware that his job was to conduct business and present performance at the "world's finest theater."

Competition was fierce in the Cleveland entertainment industry. A 1925 article in the *Plain Dealer* speculated that perhaps the city was "over seated." Loew's State had recently started programs that included films and vaudeville. Loew's had recently started its own vaudeville circuit—the corporation needed variety to fill entertainment at the more than two hundred theaters across the country. Downtown Cleveland had the Hippodrome showing variety shows, and there were numerous film theaters in the downtown area. By 1925, the Allen Theater was under the control of Loew's, as was the Stillman, Euclid and Mall Theaters. The seats needed to be filled, and John Royal was hustling to find ways to pack the Palace.

In the summer of 1925, he began to present "three a day" programs at the Palace. The thrice-daily shows included three performance rounds of Keith-Albee-Orpheum vaudeville acts supplemented with long-reel, first-run movies. Shorts had already appeared at the Palace, but first-run, long-reel movies were a new experiment.

Part of the problem for Royal was where to get the movies. In the early and late 1920s, silent movies were distributed through trusts, just as performers were signed to theatrical syndicates. Loew's theaters had a lock on Famous Players–Lasky movie productions as well as the newly created MGM productions. First National Pictures also was tied to the Loew's. In Cleveland, there was not a presence for William Fox and Fox productions. It was to Fox that the Palace turned first for long-reel movies, and in 1925, Fox's production of the *Iron Horse* was the initial offering of the three-a-day format. Royal set it up as a summer experiment. Summer came and went, and the three-a-days with a first run movie and shorts never left. The Palace Theater also began showing movies from Warner Bros. production and distribution company and used Warner Bros. as a source for movies until that company built its own theater across the street from the Palace in 1928. At the end of the decade, both vaudeville and the silent-movie industry were upended with the introduction of "talkies."

John Royal's work at the Palace did not go unnoticed. Late in 1927 and early in 1928, Edward Albee offered Royal the job of general manager of all theaters in the eastern United States outside of New York. His territory would stretch from Chicago to New Orleans across the South and through New England. At the time, Royal was quoted as saying the he "would keep

John Royal (*left*) with Johnny Burke. Royal was the first manager of Keith's Palace Theater and later worked for NBC radio and television. *Cleveland Memory Project. Cleveland State University.*

an office in Cleveland" as well as in New York. He considered himself a Clevelander and liked the city and the people.

He did not last long in the job. The change had nothing to do with his work performance. In 1928, Joseph Kennedy, the father of the future president of the United States, used his financial leverage to buy a controlling interest in the Keith-Albee-Orpheum circuit. Kennedy also got ownership of First Booking Offices of America. First Booking was a small movie production company that specialized in Westerns. With controlling interest in the seven hundred Keith-Albee-Orpheum theaters, he then fired Albee, reportedly telling him that vaudeville was out the door and Albee should leave with it.

When Kennedy took charge of Keith-Albee, he moved aggressively to build a movie distribution company. (He also merged with Pathe Exchange and Cecil B. DeMille's Producers Distributing Company.) Suddenly, Royal found himself in a business he did not know and did not fit in. Kennedy's venture lasted long enough for David Sarnoff of Radio Corporation of America to buy a controlling interest and merge everything into RKO Pictures.

Royal moved from Keith-Albee-Orpheum back to Cleveland. He was hired as the general manager of WTAM radio. At the time, WTAM was one of the most powerful stations in the Midwest. The station was the first to put a live political convention on the airwaves. In 1924, the Republican National Convention was in Cleveland, and WTAM broadcast the event live. The radio station was presenting performances of musical events at the Allen Theater as well as live broadcasts linked up with New York. Royal continued to pursue a radio schedule that had not only live musical broadcasts but also recorded music and variety acts—much like he had been arranging at the Palace Theater earlier in the decade. His success and the success of WTAM eventually led to NBC Radio buying the station. Ownership of the station brought Royal to NBC, and Royal's vaudeville connections jump-started a leadership role for NBC in headline singers and comedians in broadcasting. Those connections also led NBC to promote Royal to vice-president and director of programming. He remained at NBC until he retired in 1953 in charge of television programming.

The end of the 1920s was the beginning of great changes to the entertainment industry in general and theaters in particular. In 1927, Marcus Loew died, and he was celebrated for his life and work in newspapers around the country and especially in *Variety*. In 1927, *The Jazz Singer* arrived—a half-silent, half-talking movie starring Al Jolson. In 1928, the Cinema Theater added one last movie house to the Playhouse Square landscape. The theater was built across the street from the Palace on Euclid. It was originally an independent theater scheduled to have first-run movies but soon advertised that it specialized in second-run movies. The one-thousand-seat theater was successful at first, but the combination of the stock market crash and a controversy regarding a "travel" movie created financial hardships. The controversy surrounded a movie titled *Ingagi*, which was advertised to have been shot live in Africa. However, it was made in California and branded a fake. The gorillas in the movie were actors in suits, and one of the actors sued the production company. Several suits followed, and the costs and poor publicity caused the theater to close. In 1930, Warner Bros. bought the theater to use as a vehicle to show first-run movies for that company.

In March 1930, Edward Albee died in Palm Beach, and the legacy of B.F. Keith and the Keith Vaudeville circuit and the seven hundred Keith-Albee-Orpheum theaters passed with him. By that time, the Palace Theater was rebranded as "RKO Palace," and shortly afterward, the Allen left the Loew's group to become an RKO theater as well.

The stock market crash of 1929 placed a great deal of stress on theaters of all types, forcing some to close and many to retrofit for the new talkies. The Depression also had an impact on not only vaudeville theaters and movie houses at Playhouse Square but also legitimate theaters. It became increasingly difficult for all types of entertainment to fill the seats.

7

Changing Entertainment Options

Mayfair Casino

As the 1930s began, change was occurring at Playhouse Square. The Palace Theater, once the jewel of the Keith Vaudeville circuit, emphasized movies once it became the RKO Palace but still provided live entertainment. RKO took over the Allen in 1934 with a focus on movies and the occasional concert. The State Theater presented a mixture of movies from MGM and live performances. The Hanna and Ohio Theaters plugged away at presenting legitimate shows. Both used movies to supplement the weekly performances. Even Robert McLaughlin had a difficult time filling seats and resorted increasingly to productions from his Cleveland stock company to place entertainment on the stage. Even an appearance by Leo the Lion—the MGM mascot—in the lobby for a week promoting *Tarzan the Ape Man* could not improve the long-term prospects for the Ohio Theater. Despite all of those efforts, the Ohio closed in October 1934.

What would happen to the theater? How would Playhouse Square continue to draw people? Enter Harry Propper. A year after the Ohio closed, it returned as the Mayfair Casino.

Harry Propper was an interesting character in the Playhouse Square saga. In 1919, he opened the Claremont Tent on St. Clair Avenue with a partner, Louie Bleet. Throughout the 1920s, Propper was a bootlegger. Cleveland's access to Lake Erie provided an excellent conduit for "imported" spirits from Canada during Prohibition.

The success of the Claremont Tent venture led Propper to become associated with the Carleton Terrace—later the Band Box or Music Box Club—above the State Theater lobby at Playhouse Square, where Cleveland audiences were introduced to early swing and jazz. The Music Box Club, located at 1515 Euclid, had a hall and sponsored its own orchestra. On many nights, the Music Box Orchestra performed live for radio audiences, and the performances were broadcast throughout the Cleveland area and the Midwest. Guy Lombardo was first introduced and played at the Music Box.

In 1933, Propper took out a lease for $85,000 for a business room and basement at 1620 Euclid Avenue. The five-year lease was taken with anticipation that a new restaurant would open, as everyone was looking toward the end of Prohibition. The name would be the Mayfair Restaurant, and indeed it opened by December of that year, in time for the New Year's celebration. The Mayfair Restaurant was not the first establishment to open in the Playhouse Square area catering to theatergoers and theater people. The Monaco Restaurant was a well-established spot in the Hanna Building. Somehow, the Mayfair was different. It was large, with a dance floor, a stage and a glass-enclosed studio that served the orchestra during broadcasts on radio. The restaurant and entertainment center had two floors and stayed open late.

The restaurant was a gathering place for the well-heeled and those wanting to be near the well-heeled. When Amos 'n' Andy played the Palace Theater, the actors wandered across the street after the show to the Mayfair. There was a full-time orchestra under the direction of Michael Speciale, who gained a following and a reputation recording for the Edison and Pathe companies. Speciale also played regularly for Midwest and national radio audiences. Singers and crooners from New York and Chicago came to play the Mayfair. Propper also regularly held dance contests, and the newest dance steps could be learned and practiced on the floor.

Propper celebrated the famous who came by, and he had a fine collection of autographed photos. His upstairs office held the gallery, and he would bring vaudeville performers and theater stars up to show off. An interesting story is related by Glenn Pullen from the *Plain Dealer* of a comedian who visited the office and was complaining that the crowds "at the Palace were colder than the weather" and that another comic had come through a few weeks earlier, and the comic accused the other man of stealing his jokes. Once upstairs in Propper's office, the comic became enraged when he saw the picture and autograph of Milton Berle. According to the performer, it was Berle who had pinched his jokes.

As successful as the Mayfair Restaurant was in mid-1934, Propper had to rework his lease with Joseph Laronge Realty. The original lease had guarantees of between $1,000 and $1,500 a month and a percentage of profits. The new lease was set at $14,400 a year without a percentage, and instead of five years, the new lease would run for only one. It was still the Depression, but Harry Propper had other plans for Playhouse Square.

In 1935, Propper leased the Loew's Ohio from Loew's Ohio Theaters Incorporated under the lease name of Casino Incorporated. Under the terms, no motion pictures would be shown in the Ohio. The space would be redesigned by W.S. Ferguson, an architect and engineer and former Cleveland city service director. The cost of the redesign was over $125,000.

Included in the new space would be a theater lobby bar at least 112 feet long. Prohibition was over, and the city's theatergoers and night-clubbers would be thirsty. The stage in the auditorium was carried out 21 feet, two staircases were constructed leading to the balcony and two stairs led to the new semicircle stage. Kitchens were built under the main floor and the under the stage.

The nightclub would be able to hold 1,200 people, and the plan to provide service for the patrons was first class. A staff of 140 would be on hand for opening night. Entertainment would include Gene Baker providing music with George Duffy's and LeRoy Smith's orchestras and 20 dancing beauties and more than 30 other performers. As Propper and his co-manager, Joe Bock, prepared for opening night, they spent over $10,000 on liquor and spirits. According to one report, the first week the Mayfair was open, the business made $40,000.

In the Depression, the cost of building out the Mayfair Casino and the costs of operation were extravagant. Propper must have made a great deal of money in his previous endeavors, or Casino Inc. had deep pockets somewhere. As it turns out, he had deep-pocketed silent partners.

These partners reportedly included Moe Dalitz (once a member of a Detroit bootlegging gang), Lou Rothkopf, Morris Kleinman and Sam Tucker. Each was a member or had connections to the Mayfield Road Gang, an Italian and Russian Jewish syndicate. Bootlegging, gambling and loansharking were all part of the gang's working capital base, and the group controlled much of those activities on the east side of Cleveland. At one time, John Scalish, later the undisputed head of the Cleveland Mafia, worked at the club for $100 a week. Also connected to the Mayfair was

Cocktail lounge at the Mayfair Casino, managed by Harry Propper. *Cleveland Memory Project. Cleveland State University.*

Henry Beckerman, a mob lawyer who was the legal owner of the club's liquor license. Propper's connections in Cleveland, Chicago and New York kept the stage full and the entertainment flowing at the Mayfair. Much of the bookings were through the MCA talent agency run by Jules Stein out of Chicago. Propper's protégé Lew Wasserman eventually became an employee of MCA.

Talent bookings included Sophie Tucker, Xavier Cugat and Tommy Dorsey, as well as many other national and local bands. Propper presented lavish stage shows that included dancing women in fancy costumes, presaging those who eventually played in Las Vegas. In addition, he provided continuous entertainment with jugglers, singers and comedians. Vaudeville was losing steam at the Palace, but variety acts continued at the Mayfair. The club was advertised as the "million-dollar nightclub."

In 1936, the Republican National Convention was in Cleveland, at Public Auditorium. At that convention, the Republicans nominated Alf Landon to run against Franklin Delano Roosevelt. The Mayfair Casino

Performers at the Mayfair Casino. The Mayfair had elaborate stage shows in 1934–35. *Cleveland Memory Project. Cleveland State University.*

was one of the places where delegates could relax and enjoy themselves after the floor work was completed for the night. Special one-way traveling restrictions on Euclid Avenue were put in place due to the large number of vehicles that stopped at Playhouse Square in general and Mayfair Casino specifically during the convention.

Despite the notoriety and success of the casino, by December 1936, the Mayfair had gone bankrupt. Propper left the Mayfair in November to travel to Florida due to health reasons. At that time, the nightclub was supposed to be taken over by the French Casino chain of New York and Lew Wasserman was to be installed as manager. The deal fell through, and Durries (Duke) Crane, a restaurateur, became the operator in December. Crane's enterprise lasted a little over two months, and the Durries Crane Corporation filed for bankruptcy.

Once again, Propper was brought back to run the cabaret and nightclub, now being operated by Euclid Casino Inc. with Nate Wiesenberg as president. Wiesenberg was known as the "slots king" of northeast Ohio. The grand reopening of the Mayfair once again had "regular prices" and lavish stage shows and big bands performing. America was still in the throes of the Depression. The reopening and new ownership lasted only until December 1937, when once again the company filed for bankruptcy.

Throughout the two-year run of the Mayfair Casino, Cleveland police staged raids targeting illegal gaming activities. The raids never resulted in an arrest, despite the firm belief by authorities and Cleveland's safety director, Eliot Ness, that something unsavory was taking place.

Harry Propper moved to Miami once the Mayfair closed for good in December 1937 but returned to Cleveland, where he died in 1939. Moe Dalitz, his original investment partner, ended up in Las Vegas and owned the Desert Inn Resort and Casino and helped finance the Showboat and Stardust Casinos. Dalitz was known as "Mr. Las Vegas" and was influential in the growth and development of the city. Durries Duke Crane went on to become a head chef at the Palmer House in Chicago, director of food concessions for military installations at the request of Secretary of War Henry L. Stimpson in 1943 and then president of National Food Corporation. Nate Wiesenberg continued to be involved with slot machines in Cleveland and was found shot to death in Cleveland Heights in 1945.

Once the Mayfair Casino closed, the lights were dimmed at the Ohio for the remainder of the 1930s. Playhouse Square itself continued to provide entertainment both in the theaters and around the square.

ALPINE VILLAGE RESTAURANT

About the time the Mayfair Casino opened, Herman Pirchner opened the Alpine Village Restaurant. When the Mayfair closed, the Village was well on the way to a thirty-year stretch at Playhouse Square.

Herman Pirchner emigrated from Austria to Cleveland in the 1920s. Upon arriving, he worked two jobs, one being a busboy. He briefly brewed beer with his brothers in defiance of Prohibition but quickly got out of the business when Cleveland Mafia members tried to obtain part of the action. Opening the Lake Shore Club in the late 1920s, he got into the restaurant business. The Lake Shore Club was reported to have a speakeasy within the building. When the Lake Shore Club closed, he opened the Alpine Village.

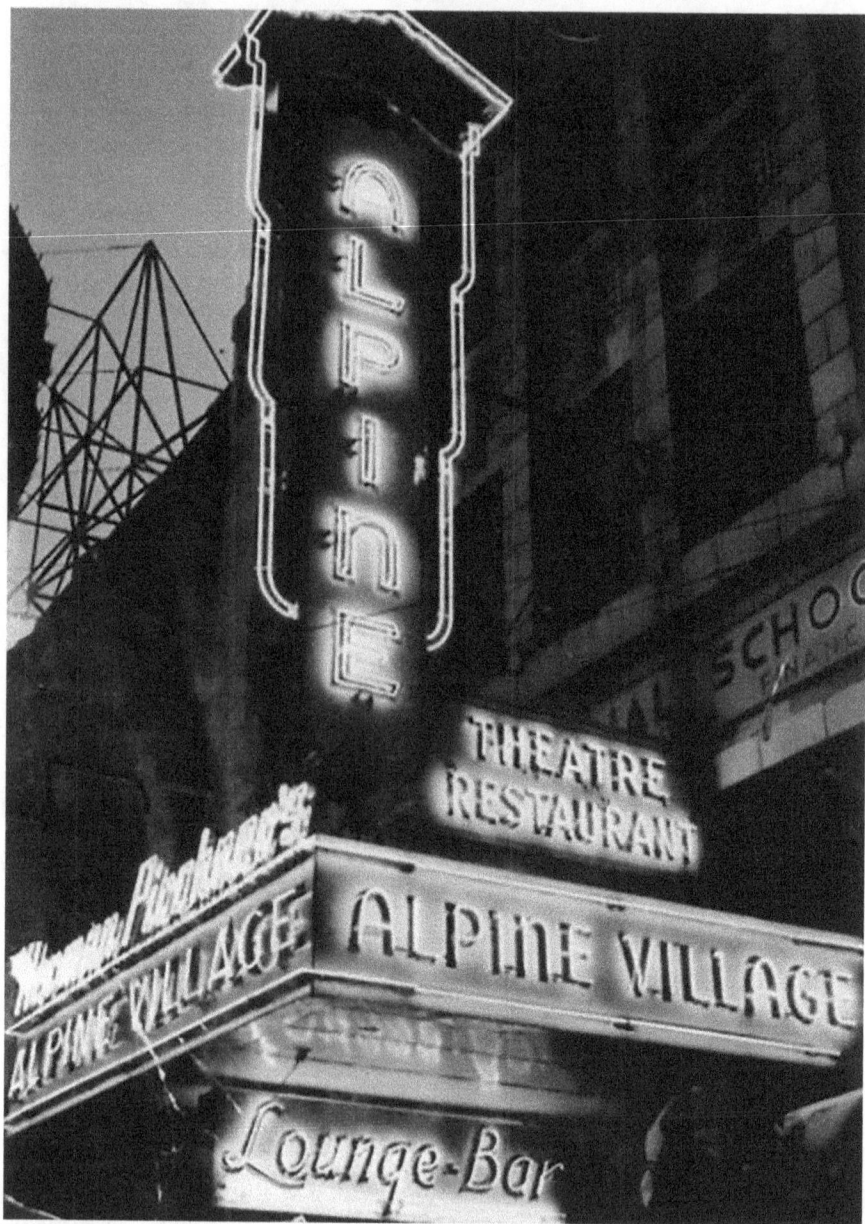

Outside signage for the Alpine Village on Euclid Avenue. The Village was open from 1934 until 1961. *Cleveland Memory Project. Cleveland State University.*

Herman Pirchner, owner of the Alpine Village Restaurant, holding fifty-six sixteen-ounce steins of beer without a tray, part of his showmanship at the restaurant. *Cleveland Memory Project. Cleveland State University.*

Pirchner was a real showman, having gained experience as an aerialist, clown and wrestler back in Austria. At the Alpine Village, he dressed in leather shorts and a Tyrolean cap. He led German sing-alongs and yodeled. He gave rolling pins to new brides and slid across the floor delivering steins of beer to patrons. He was in *Ripley's Believe It or Not!* in 1933 because of his beer hefting. The restaurant eventually built an upstairs private club called Eldorado, where visiting stars from Playhouse Square such as Bob Hope and Frank Sinatra would gather.

Once the Mayfair Casino closed for good, Pirchner put on floor shows that included dancers and big-time musicians and comedians. Stars such as Pearl Bailey, Jimmy Durante and Cab Calloway performed at the Alpine Village. Swing was king, and the supper club grew in stature and outlasted many of the entertainment venues that cropped up around Playhouse Square and the general Cleveland area. Pirchner grew in his role not only as owner of an entertainment center but also as a community leader. During the war years, he led war bond drives and supported many local charity and civic events. He even produced his own shows that were presented at Public Hall and Playhouse Square theaters. Finally, in 1961, the Alpine Village was forced to close due to bankruptcy. The Internal Revenue Service padlocked the restaurant. Herman Pirchner died in 2009 at the age of 101 in Lakewood, Ohio. Where the Alpine Village was located, a parking lot emerged.

8

WELCOME MR. FIRST-NIGHTER

I n the 1940s, Playhouse Square continued to provide entertainment for Clevelanders. The Palace Theater regularly provided live shows with big swing bands and movies as a double feature. The State was primarily showing movies. The Allen Theater was a movie-only showhouse. Warner Bros. moved uptown to the Hippodrome and left the Lake Theater to show B movies as long as it could; the theater went dark for many weeks. The Ohio briefly opened up as a P.T. Barnum–style museum showing oddities from around the world before reopening in 1943 under the leadership of Gertrude Tracy. She was the first woman to supervise a theater in Cleveland. The Hanna Theater continued to provide legitimate stage shows, dramas and musicals through the Schubert Booking agency as long as and whenever shows traveled outside of New York.

Entertainment continued around the square as the Alpine Village gained momentum and the Eldorado club upstairs opened and gained notoriety. The Village added a stage that rose from the floor, and the floor shows got bigger. Above the State Theater, the Stage Door Canteen opened up where once the Music Box Club of Harry Propper existed. The Canteen opened in 1943 and, running on donations, provided a place where servicemen in a strange city could find food, entertainment and people. It was one of eight in the country and was operated by the American Theater Wing.

In 1941, the Hanna Theater hired Milton Krantz to be the new manager. Originally from Chicago, Krantz began his theater work at thirteen selling candy at Chicago's Studebaker Theater. He was loud and persuasive,

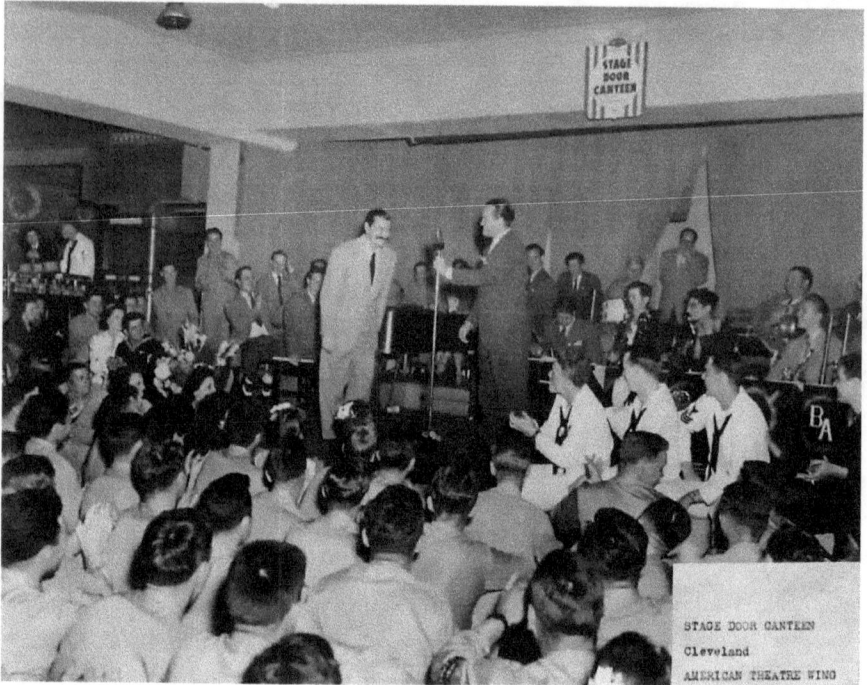

Bob Hope (*right*) and Jerry Colonna at the Stage Door Canteen in Cleveland, Ohio. *Billy Rose Theatre Division, New York Public Library Digital Collection.*

setting a record for candy sales. It was because of selling candy that he was encouraged to become a theater promoter. Selling chocolate candy was no different than selling stage plays, according to a theater house manager. Within a few short years, Krantz was the head of the Studebaker Theater. When he received the top job at the Hanna, he became the youngest manager of a major theater in the country.

Krantz's experiences leading up to the Hanna Theater job included being stage manager at the Illinois Theater and working as an assistant to Erlanger Productions. During that time, he became friends with Flo Ziegfeld. He also got to know the Lunts (Alfred Lunt and Lynn Fontanne) when he handled their company Amphtrion 38 when touring Texas in 1938.

Krantz was an energetic and electric showman, even though he never played on the stage. He was open to modern ideas surrounding the theater and was always willing and interested in promoting increased attendance. In late 1941, just after being hired at the Hanna, Krantz, responding to a question about the dress requirements at the theater, said, "I would rather see a theater full of people in street clothes really enjoying a drama than as a silk hat crowd filling only half a house." His response was in answer to a question by the public trying to determine if buying gowns and tails would put going out to see a show beyond financial reach. His answer was a bit of heresy for old-line theatergoers, but it set the stage for Krantz's approach to filling the seats.

Krantz wasted little time setting the stage and filling the seats as he negotiated contracts with the American Theater Society and the Theater Guild of New York to create the first subscription series. Those contracts allowed an impressive array of stars to come through Cleveland. Stars such as Katharine Hepburn, Ethel Barrymore and the Lunts made regular appearances during his early tenure at the Hanna

Never one to rest on his laurels, Krantz made regular trips to New York and Chicago to work with producers to bring top shows into Cleveland. He operated as many of the original theater managers did in the 1920s, as the primary booking agent for stage productions at the Hanna. Along the way, he added Richard Rodgers and Oscar Hammerstein to his list of friends, and the friendship paid off for Cleveland theatergoers. Krantz was able to bring some of the biggest productions into the city through his connections. Shows such as *Oklahoma!*, *South Pacific*, *The King and I* and *The Sound of Music* made it to the Cleveland stage. Some were so large and lavish that Krantz brokered deals for Cleveland's Music Hall to host many of the larger shows. The Music Hall had a larger seating capacity than the Hanna, and Krantz was the manager of record through the Hanna to present and produce shows at the bigger theater.

Krantz's showmanship was not above getting publicity from odd places if it sold seats. He had Bill Veeck, the owner of the Cleveland Indians, guest star in a production at the Hanna. Veeck was also a great promoter who once brought in a three-foot, seven-inch player to pinch-hit in a major league game. Veeck signed Larry Doby, the American league's first African American player, and he owned the 1948 World Series Championship team in Cleveland. He was not a good actor. However, Krantz was out to sell seats during the slow summer stock season, and Veeck's appearance did just that.

Starting in the late 1940s and continuing into the early 1950s, booking road shows became more difficult. Krantz worked overtime to bring quality theater and top stars to the Hanna. The late 1940s was some of the best revenue years ever for the Hanna, with show-stopping runs by *Oklahoma!*, *South Pacific* and *Annie Get Your Gun*. Despite the success and the demand from Cleveland audiences, Broadway producers wanted larger guarantees and more profit from road shows. The guarantees meant that bringing Broadway to Cleveland was becoming harder to accomplish. The cost of sending a show on the road was becoming frightfully high.

As early as 1950, Milton Krantz was at the forefront of a plan to organize independent theaters around the country. An initial meeting in Pittsburgh at the start of 1951 was followed up in December of that year in Cleveland. The plan was to have audiences subscribe to road-show series supported by the New York Theater Guild and the American Theater Society sponsored by the Council of Living Theater. Subscriptions from around the country would create a pool of money that could then be used to support touring Broadway shows. Cleveland audiences were already familiar with subscriptions to the theater, as they had been spearheaded by Krantz in the 1940s.

Enter the U.S. Supreme Court. In 1955, a civil antitrust action initiated by the government was brought against the Schubert Theatrical Company for violating the Sherman Anti-Trust Act. In the complaint, the Schubert organization was found guilty of business policies that limited competition through producing, booking and presenting legitimate theatrical productions

Broadway executives promoting subscriptions to the Hanna Theater. *Cleveland Memory Project. Cleveland State University.*

across many states. An end to the stranglehold on bookings through the Schubert organization was the result. The Hanna's association with the Schubert Theatrical organization went back to the opening of the theater in 1921. The Schuberts were one of two legitimate theatrical booking companies. The other was Erlanger and Klaw, which supplied shows to the Ohio Theater. Erlanger and Klaw broke up after the death of Abe Erlanger in the 1930s. The Schubert organization continued, and the company was then known as Select Theater Corporation and United Booking. Not only did the Schubert organization produce shows, but it was also a realty company owning hundreds of theaters around the United States. A Schubert-produced show would start in a Schubert theater in New York. If it went on the road, the show would go to a Schubert road theater. The Hanna was not a Schubert-owned theater. It was an independent theater, so the likelihood that a Schubert show would land in Cleveland with any frequency was slim.

Milton Krantz, having already invested time and energy in the Theater Guild subscription project, now became a leader in another effort to supply quality theater both for the Hanna and for other tour cities. Once the Schubert organization folded in 1956, Krantz became a prime player in creating the League of New York Theaters. The national booking service enlisted eighty of Broadway's leading producers as part of the Independent Booking Office with the goal of providing weekly engagements to theater lovers across the United States and Canada.

In 1958, Krantz and the Hanna Theater became a testing ground for minimum two-week show engagements. The experiment was aimed at creating publicity buzz for road shows and increasing theater subscriptions. Krantz's energy and promotional wizardry pushed the plan over the top, to the benefit of Cleveland's Hanna Theater primarily but also eventually to theater managers everywhere. The main points of the plan were salesmanship and aggressive marketing. The "new" plan simply became an extension of the twenty-year-old Theater Guild subscription plan Krantz first developed, called the Hanna Plan. The organization formally became the Legitimate Independent (in some circles International) Theater Managers Association (LITMA).

A transcontinental circuit reminiscent of the Erlanger and Klaw Syndicate and the Keith Circuit of years before was envisioned. The first year of the circuit enlisted Washington, Philadelphia, Detroit, Chicago, Los Angeles, San Francisco and Cleveland. Guaranteeing two-week stops at each theater in the circuit reduced costs to the show's producer and opened possibilities for group sales during the second (or third) week of the show. It also effectively doubled the number of available seats for Theater Guild subscribers.

The plan proved a success, with the number of Cleveland subscribers nearing ten thousand and the number of cities entering into LITMA growing to twenty-three. The success of the plan allowed for smaller touring cities to participate and smaller shows to get stage opportunities outside of New York. Although successful, the plan did not overcome the critical issue of New York money backing theater ventures. The lingering question was, Did all shows have to originate in New York for touring to be profitable?

Milton Krantz was not to be stymied by New York money woes. He was always looking for a way to keep the seats filled. At the Hanna, he installed a new speaker system, allowing patrons to better hear stage performers and movie sounds on a larger movie screen. He instituted a film festival at the Hanna. He made connections with other theater groups and stock companies around the country, including the Signet Group and the Royal Poinciana Theater in Palm Beach, Florida, to extend performance weeks. All the deal making, promotions and interconnections with New York producers and actors were not Milton Krantz's best help to Playhouse Square. Krantz himself was, for he was "Mr. First-Nighter."

At the start of every run of performances, he would dress in a dinner jacket and greet patrons entering the theater (many by their first name) and make all feel as if they were truly welcome. He would move through the aisles and shake hands and reintroduce or introduce himself to the audience. The Hanna Theater was their theater. He could take poorly written shows and make a profitable run in Cleveland, because he knew his audience and knew how to make people feel comfortable and welcome at the theater. This was true for the subscriber of many years or the first-time theatergoer. He was the guardian of the theater for more than forty-two years in Cleveland. His experiences would make for a good drama or an entertaining comedy.

Examples of his concern for the theatergoing audience are renowned. In 1944–45, Krantz regularly invited military patients from Crile Hospital to the Hanna. A bus would be sent to the hospital to pick up the soldiers, take them to dine at the Carter Hotel and, after the show, bring them to Otto Moser's for a sandwich and beer. Krantz wanted these men to experience theater and what an evening at the Hanna was all about. On one occasion, a man attending his first legitimate theater performance mistakenly thought that the experience would be like going to the movies—he would see the first show and then stay for the second, as one would do at a local movie house. Instead of having the man leave, Krantz arranged for the man and

Milton Krantz, "Mr. First-Nighter," in front of the Hanna Theater. *Cleveland Press photographer, Bernie Noble. Cleveland Memory Project. Cleveland State University.*

his wife to stay for the second show. One evening, a man got sick from the balcony and threw up on the patrons below. After the ensuing commotion, two women had to have their fur coats sent out to the cleaners—all at Krantz and the Hanna's expense.

Krantz was the manager of the Hanna Theater for forty-two years. He was not just the theater manager but also the managing director of the Hanna starting in 1960. He experienced a robbery at the theater, many medical emergencies (his brother was a doctor, and Krantz knew a great deal of first aid) and a bombing during the run of *Hair*, all the while continually working to improve the shows and build the audience for the Hanna. He was friend and acquaintance to many of Broadway's biggest performers and the longest-serving theater manager in the country. In fact, he entered the Guinness World Records for his length of stay at one theater.

Perhaps his most classic gift to Cleveland was the Hanna curtain. Starting about 1949, stage mementos began appearing on the back of the

Godspell cast adding the logo to the play on the back of the Hanna curtain. *Cleveland Memory Project. Cleveland State University.*

curtain. Over time, it grew from a few notes and cartoons to a treasure of stage history. Just about every show and star that performed at the Hanna over thirty years has representation. When Krantz retired in 1982, the treasured curtain was retired as well. After some frantic searching, the curtain is now firmly in the safekeeping of Cleveland State University. The forty-by-forty-foot curtain is not on display, but the memories are kept with the goal of someday being able to show the world a treasured piece of theater history.

Milton Krantz remained in Cleveland after retiring from the Hanna. His notes from forty-two years as manager of the Hanna could fill a book. He died in 2006 at the age of ninety-four at his home in Beachwood, Ohio.

9

A Tale of Two Anniversaries

In 1946 and 1947, the world was adjusting to the end of the Second World War. Servicemen were returning home, and the country was beginning a return to normal life. Playhouse Square was about to celebrate twenty-five years of entertainment in Cleveland. The grand theaters were open once again. The Palace Theater was still the RKO Palace, and although vaudeville and variety shows were no longer the rage, double features often included a performance by a big band on stage and a movie. The Allen Theater was also an RKO theater, and its manager was Howard Higley, at the theater since 1934.

Higley was born in the Cleveland area and, while attending Shaw High School, began working as an usher at the RKO Palace Theater. After graduation, he was moved to the Hippodrome Theater, where he became an assistant manager. When the Hippodrome changed ownership as a Warner Bros. theater, he returned to the Palace and also spent time working at Keith's 105 Street Theater. In 1934, the Allen Theater became an RKO-Warner theater, and it was there that Higley began a long run as manager. Higley had a front-row seat to the changes and struggles at Playhouse Square through the Depression, the war and the celebration year (and beyond).

The State Theater and the Ohio were open and still under the management of Loew's Theaters. The State had operated continuously throughout the 1930s and '40s, and the Ohio reopened in 1943 under the guidance of Gertrude Tracy. In fact, Loew's still had a number of first-run movie theaters in the downtown area. Loew's would try to maximize first-run movie time by creating a "move over" policy within the three downtown theaters it controlled. A film would open to great fanfare at the State or Stillman and then move over to the Ohio Theater or to one of the other Loew's theaters to create multiple weeks of exclusive first-run presentations.

The Lake Theater was closed many weeks during the 1940s as Warner Bros. moved to use the Hippodrome as the first-run movie theater in downtown Cleveland. In 1948, the Lake was sold and reopened as a smaller, 701-seat independent venue renamed the Esquire Theater.

The Hanna Theater was still presenting legitimate theater under the guidance of Milton Krantz and still filling seats with big-name stars and big-name shows. The stars included Mary Martin, Joe E. Brown, Tallulah Bankhead and the magician Blackstone. The shows included *Annie Get Your Gun*, *Private Lives* and *Oklahoma!*

Herman Pirchner's Alpine Village was the place to be for entertainment around Playhouse Square. However, the Stage Door Canteen closed after the war, and the space above the State Theater where the canteen existed was filled by the Cleveland Recording Company. The recording company, begun in 1938 by Frederick Wolf, was the first professional recording studio in Cleveland. Wolf used the company to open several radio stations all headquartered at the same location and, after the Stage Door Canteen closed, moved everything to Playhouse Square. The radio stations included WCCR (AM) and WDOK (both AM and FM). Over time, the studio under the leadership of Ken Hamann built a state-of-the-art mastering facility. Many notable hit records were produced at the studio. Eventually, Hamann and a production engineer, John Hansen, purchased Cleveland Recording Company from Frederick Wolf, and the studio moved from above the State Theater farther up Euclid Avenue.

Celebrations for the twenty-fifth anniversary of Playhouse Square and the Playhouse theaters were muted for the State, Ohio and Allen Theaters. Howard Higley prepared for the anniversary with a first-run film, *Tarzan* starring Johnny Weissmuller (who had a remarkable seventy-five lines throughout the entire movie). Higley also promoted a Saturday-afternoon cartoon festival, where children were entertained by three hours of animation.

The next year, the Palace Theater got some good news with the arrival of Danny Kaye to the theater as part of the anniversary celebration. It was the only theater to host a heavily promoted anniversary event.

A true supporter of vaudeville, Danny Kaye expanded his talents into legitimate theater and movies and was deemed the best performer to help celebrate the original roots of the Palace Theater. The show featured Georgia Gibbs; the Tip, Tap, and Toe dancers; puppets; and several other

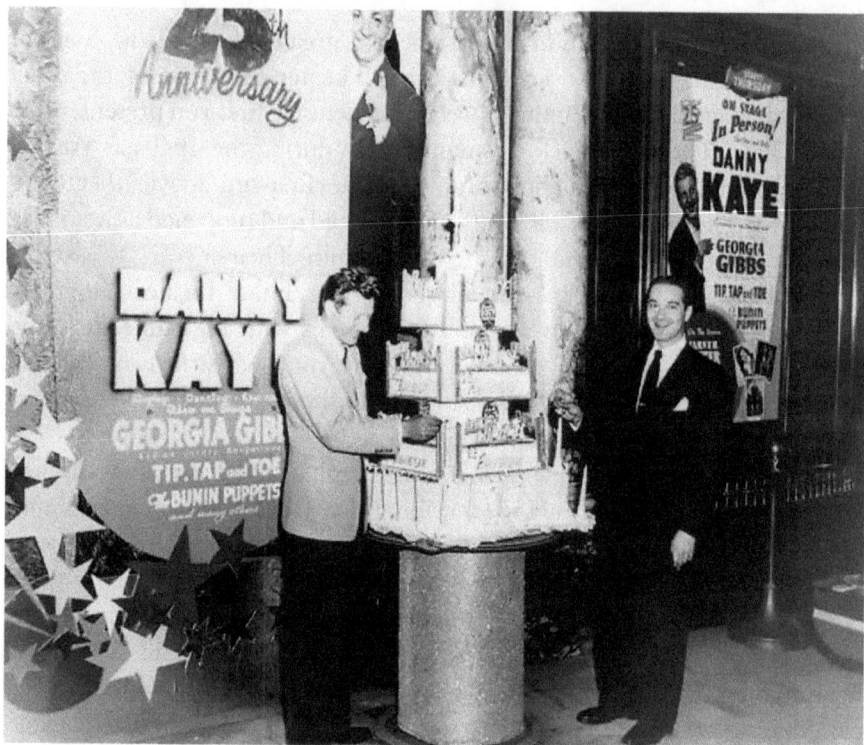

Danny Kaye at the twenty-fifth anniversary of the Palace Theater. *Cleveland Memory Project. Cleveland State University.*

variety acts. Continuous vaudeville had disappeared from the Palace stage by the early 1930s, supplemented by a combined stage and film bill. *The Danny Kaye Show* was also supported by a movie between shows.

Patrons arriving at the Palace anniversary celebration could enter for free if they presented the ticket from the first night at the theater. Much of what they saw during the twenty-fifth anniversary celebration was little different from the opening night. The hand-weaved Czechoslovakian carpet, the marbled covered walls and the vast painting and art collection on the Palace walls were still in place. An evening out at the Palace still had echoes of the "finest theater in the world."

Backstage remained well appointed, with seven stories of dressing rooms with individual baths and relaxation areas for performers on the other side of the stage. Few live performances were held at the Palace, so the backstage area was little used. However, Kaye and his troupe could relax and prepare in style between shows.

Movies became the biggest draw for patrons at the large Playhouse Square theaters. But three areas of competition for the moviegoing public's ticket money and significant demographic changes would create ongoing issues for downtown theaters over the next twenty-five years. In the 1930s, there were no more than thirty suburban theaters awaiting the release of B movies or the movement of first-run shows from the major theaters in Cleveland. The major theater chains controlled the distribution of movies as well as the production of movies. MGM was still associated with Loew's Theaters. RKO owned a movie production company and hundreds of theaters around the country. Warner Bros. also had many theaters that were the outlets for first-run movies. Through vertical integration (effectively monopolies), the major theater studios were able to control the distribution of first-run movies and therefore control the sales of tickets. By the 1940s, there were fifty-three suburban theaters. These theaters were drawing more moviegoers and placing greater demands on the major studios to release first-run movies more widely.

In 1948, a Supreme Court decision, *U.S. v Paramount Pictures et al.*, accused movie production studios of violating the Sherman Anti-Trust Act. The violation was that the major movie studios controlled most of the country's movie theaters. The relief being asked by the government was that the studios end block booking (independent theater owners had to sign contracts requiring a set number of films) and get rid of the distribution theaters under the studios' control. The decision resulted in consent decrees that ended block booking and the divestiture of theater chains. MGM-Loew's, Warner Bros., RKO and Paramount and 20th Century Fox had to get rid of the theaters they owned.

The net effect in Cleveland was that Playhouse Square theaters would no longer be affiliated with the major movie theaters, and the number of suburban theaters in the 1950s exploded to more than seventy, with an additional twenty-seven drive-in theaters around the area. First-run movies were still played at Playhouse Square. However, they also played in the surrounding suburbs. The Allen Theater, under Higley's experienced hand, continued to find some success as a first-run house for Columbia Pictures and Warner Bros. productions. He also started featuring long road-show runs. First-run movies would be booked at the Allen for multiple weeks and exclusive performances.

Higley was the last of the active managers who not only was on site to supervise the theater during performances but also had responsibility for booking movies, advertising and marketing. He presented movies and mixed in live acts and contests, designed to bring patrons downtown to the theater during the up-and-down years of the 1950s and '60s.

In order to meet the competition from surrounding suburban theaters, Playhouse Square installed larger screens, air-conditioning and updated projection equipment (70 millimeter). Cinerama was set up at the State and Palace Theaters late in the 1950s. Cinerama used a wraparound, widescreen format with multitrack stereo sound. CinemaScope was also introduced using 70-millimeter projection equipment. The Allen was one of the first venues to install these upgraded systems during renovations, one in 1953 and again eight years later. The 1961 renovations restored the Allen rotunda and cost an estimated $300,000. At first, only the largest theaters could present movies in these formats, and crowds were persuaded to come downtown to Playhouse Square.

The Ohio Theater joined the Allen in becoming a long-run movie house. Management at the Ohio signed exclusive first-run movie contracts for extended periods of time. This was a return to a place the Ohio held in the mid-1920s. Movies such as *Ten Commandments* and *Ben-Hur* were road-show hits in the 1920s and returned with remakes for long engagements starting in the mid-1950s. The *Ten Commandments* played for twenty-nine weeks. *Ben-Hur* played for forty-eight. In the 1960s, the road-show engagements continued; *The Sound of Music* topped all performances with a ninety-one-week run. The other Playhouse Square theaters also practiced "hold-over" movies for first-run engagements, enough that W. Ward Marsh, the *Plain Dealer's* movie critic, commented in 1959 that theater managers were enthusiastic about the future. The investments in larger screens and better projection equipment held the decline at bay for a bit longer.

Television was also on the rise. In 1948, seventy-two thousand television sets were sold in the United States at an average cost of $1,200. Only 9 percent of American households owned a TV in 1950, but by the end of the decade, 85 percent of American families had a television set. And the average cost of a set dropped to $600. The breakup of the studio system opened up avenues for movie production companies to get into the television business. Releasing movies for viewing on TV provided another revenue stream for the studios and an option for the movie-viewing public to watch the stars other than going out to a downtown theater.

Finally, the expansion of the suburbs around Cleveland fueled an abandonment of the central city entertainment area. First-run movies were soon seen in the local suburban neighborhood theater. There was no need to travel downtown. The Hanna presented live theater, which was unique and could not be replicated in the suburbs. It was able to survive, though with difficulty and through the effort of Milton Krantz. However, the other great theaters of Playhouse Square were finding fewer and fewer patrons. This was despite the success of the Ohio Theater in presenting long-run road-show hits. Even Howard Higley moved to the suburbs. In 1966, after thirty-four years as manager of the Allen Theater, he became the full-time manager for the Stanley-Warner Great Northern Theater in the suburbs.

Without the support and deep financial pockets of major movie studios, maintenance and upkeep of the large theaters at Playhouse Square fell to individual theater management. The result was delayed upkeep and a downward trend in looks and accommodations.

Other intervening factors in the 1960s were racial segregation, poverty concentrated in the inner city and racial unrest finally exploding in several days of riots in Cleveland, creating a safety vacuum in downtown. Many suburbanites continued to work downtown, but by 5:00 p.m. they left for home outside of the central city. People did not feel safe in the city after work or in the evening. More commuters created demand for more parking, and as Cleveland planned urban renewal projects in the late 1950s and early '60s, parking replaced buildings over vast stretches of the city.

The net effects of these factors were fewer patrons and financial hardships for Playhouse Square. A fire did not help.

On July 5, 1964, a fire started in the grand lobby of the Ohio Theater, destroying the entrance. A maintenance worker discovered the fire and alerted authorities—otherwise, the damage, which was extensive, could have been much worse. Gone were the exquisite lobby murals, coiffured ceiling and chandeliers. The carpeting had to be removed; even the mezzanine area was damaged. Adding insult to injury, the fire occurred after the Ohio had recently completed a renovation. A temporary repair hid the damage using drywall and creating an art deco façade. The Ohio did recover, due in great part to two long-run bookings of Julie Andrews's movies *Mary Poppins*, lasting thirteen weeks, and *The Sound of Music*.

The grand theaters of Playhouse Square found upkeep and operation more and more difficult. Once suburban theaters began booking long-run road shows and first-run movies, even the Ohio and Allen began the short road to financial ruin. One by one, the great Playhouse Square theaters closed.

The Esquire Theater had closed back in 1951 but found new life as a television studio. Another remodel downsized the theater to a three-hundred-person-capacity venue for WXEL, which would later become WJW-TV.

Ohio lobby fire in July 1964. *Cleveland Public Library Photograph Collection.*

The Allen was next, although the closing came about in spurts. In March 1968, the Allen closed the first time. However, a lease with the owners of the Bulkley Building was in effect until 1971. The theater reopened, closed and opened again, eventually closing for good in May 1968. The theater itself was rented on a nightly event option basis, hosting concerts through 1968 and into 1970. The concerts benefited from the amazing acoustics initially built into the Allen's design by C. Howard Crane. Jefferson Airplane, the Doors and an R&B-soul revue featuring Jackie Wilson were among the headliners on the Allen stage after the theater finally closed in 1968.

The State and the Ohio Theaters closed early in 1969. The same issues that impacted the Allen worked to push patrons away from the two former Loew's theaters. The last of the grand theaters to open was the last to

Above: Palace Theater marquee during the last movie prior to closing, due to the air-conditioning system breaking down. Cleveland Press *photographer, Tom Prusha. Cleveland Memory Project. Cleveland State University.*

Right: Marquee of the Ohio Theater sitting vacant after the theaters closed. *Cleveland Memory Project. Cleveland State University.*

close. The air-conditioning failed at the Palace Theater during a showing of *Krakatoa, East of Java* on July 20, 1969. The Palace closed its doors, as management elected not to invest in a new air-conditioning system.

The closing of the Palace left the Hanna as the last remaining theater in the Playhouse Square area. Milton Krantz was ending a successful season and, late in the summer, announced nine shows, including four musicals for the 1969–70 season. As the other theaters closed, the entertainment options around Playhouse Square also contracted. The Alpine Village closed in 1961 as crowds diminished. Two other ventures at the same location—the Americana Supper Club and Casey's Stardust Lounge—opened and closed along with the theaters.

The fiftieth anniversary of the Playhouse Square approached with the four theaters on Euclid Avenue closed and boarded up. Two years short of the fiftieth anniversary, the blocks along Euclid between Fourteenth and Seventeenth Streets became a deserted stretch in the evenings. The restaurants and entertainment venues around the theaters closed, and the prospects for reopening or revitalization dimmed. Cleveland was looking for more commuter parking, and the theaters just might fit the bill.

10

REBIRTH

The closing of the major theaters along Euclid Avenue sent shockwaves through businesses around them and created stress among city leaders. The announcement of the Palace shutting its doors was a catalyst behind a merchants association called 9-18 Corp and the exploration of a consortium between the Greater Cleveland Growth Association and the City of Cleveland to start something in and around Playhouse Square. The merchants group put together a sidewalk art sale in the Playhouse Square area, and the new owners of the Ohio and State Theaters, Mike Miller and Benjamin Cappadora, actively sought pitches from interested parties. The interests were all nontheatrical. The owners felt that the State and the Palace would never be used again as theaters. The Ohio had promise, as it was smaller. But time passed by for large, 2,500-seat theaters. Cappadora was also engaged in putting together the financing to purchase the Bulkley Building, which included the Allen Theater.

Options for renewal were limited, despite the fact that there was early interest by Cleveland's foundations to award money to an undertaking at Playhouse Square. The undertaking would have to proceed with some speed, because it would not take long for an unused section of a downtown area to begin to look seedy. Once that happens, people completely stay away.

The rebirth and steady rise of Playhouse Square can be divided into three acts. The first was the vision and energy of Ray Shepardson, who initiated the Playhouse Square Association and gathered a group of volunteers and supporters to begin the process. The second was the savvy experience and restoration push pursued by Larry Wilker, who took over after Shepardson. The third act was the growth and program development conducted by Art Falco. The coda is still being written as Playhouse Square begins its second century.

Ray Shepardson—Visionary

Ray K. Shepardson was a young man from Seattle, Washington. He came to Cleveland in 1968, working for the Cleveland Public Schools as an assistant to Paul Briggs, superintendent of schools. Part of his job was to help recruit new teachers for the school district. The district required space for new teachers to gather, and that led Shepardson to the State Theater. The date was February 5, 1970, and his life began to change that day. The auditorium was stripped of furniture, but the lobby with the James Daugherty murals still had a Versaillian aura about it. As the story goes, Shepardson was at his barbershop four weeks later and saw an issue of *Life* magazine featuring the Daugherty murals on the cover. It was a sign from the heavens. The change in Ray's life was complete.

Shepardson moved into the Chesterfield Apartments and at the end of the school year quit his job. Using his contacts with news organizations established while at Cleveland Municipal Schools, he started to shout out the need to save Playhouse Square. In July 1970, he formed the Playhouse Square Association and began recruiting volunteers and supporters. Stints on local radio programs, noontime talks to the local Kiwanis Club and Rotary Club and visits with the Intown women's club stirred the waters. An eclectic and important group of interested individuals coalesced.

Shepardson approached the task of reopening the theaters with a missionary zeal. As part of the initial hook for financial support, he offered lifetime memberships to the Playhouse Square Association for the first two thousand people who paid $120. He admitted later that the idea was not a good business plan, but he was not a businessman, and he really needed to get the word out that the need for cash was dire and time was of the essence.

Using the seed money from association membership, Shepardson began looking for space and an event. His first efforts turned to the Allen Theater. He arranged with the Millcap Corporation, owners of the Allen, to allow him to open the theater for shows on a rental basis. The Allen was not in bad shape, and with a bit of cleaning it could be readied for a performance. The arrangement was for the ticket proceeds to cover the rent and the concession sales to go to the association. The first event was a performance by the Budapest Symphony Orchestra. Shepardson had help from Zoltan Gambos.

Zoltan Gambos was the publisher of a Hungarian daily paper, *Szabadsag*. He arrived in Cleveland in 1925 and graduated from Western Reserve University in 1929. He worked his way up the newspaper hierarchy, from sports columnist to city editor and then managing editor. Eventually, he became president of Liberty Publishing Company and acquired several other Hungarian-language newspapers. When Shepardson formed the Playhouse Square Association, Gambos was one of the founding members. Gambos strongly believed that a city could not continue to be successful without entertainment downtown, and he no doubt remembered the glory years of the downtown theaters.

The plan was to heavily advertise the arrival of the Budapest Symphony within the Hungarian community around Cleveland. Gambos guaranteed the costs to present the orchestra and underwrote the entire project. Additionally, he turned over any profits to the Playhouse Square Association. The performance was a sellout success and demonstrated that Clevelanders would come back downtown—even on a cold evening.

The real trick was to build on the success of the orchestra performance. The Sierra Leone Dance Company was next and drew ten thousand people. However, it was not a financial success. Nor was the Hungarian movie *Adrift*. Fortunately, the movie production company donated a great deal of promotional money to help pull off the event. Again, Gambos was the financial backer and local promoter. Shepardson was also able to get some financial support from the 9-18 Corporation.

Shepardson's master plan for Playhouse Square included using the Allen Theater as a multiplex movie theater. He had already invested several thousand dollars on new projection equipment as he readied the Allen for the presentation of *Adrift*. He saw the Palace as a concert hall, the Ohio as legitimate theater once again and the State as a multiuse nightclub, restaurant and banquet hall. The ideas and vision were present, but major corporate financial support was not.

In 1972, the Playhouse Square Association had a staff of six: Shepardson; maintenance man Ralph Smith; Bert LeGrande, in charge of memberships; Victor Villimas, who ran the box office and anything else needed at a given moment; a man who worked in community relations; and Ceil Hartman (the future Mrs. Shepardson), who tripled as secretary, promotion assistant and bookkeeper. Besides the paid staff, Shepardson gathered volunteers from service organizations and Cleveland State University, as well as individuals willing to help out to save the theaters.

In March, the association planned on putting on a performance by Richard Harris. At that time, a young volunteer by the name of Frank Dutton came down to the Allen Theater to help out wherever he could. The night of the performance, Shepardson had Dutton dusting off seats and filling popcorn boxes when suddenly Shepardson told Dutton that he was in charge of the concession stand in the mezzanine. When summer rolled around, the high school student was answering phones, working on the theater roof and running the box office. For Dutton, it was the start of a multiyear stint volunteering and working at Playhouse Square. Shepardson was willing to take help and place anyone in positions of responsibility. His organizational mantra was "eclectic chaos."

An important admirer early on was Mrs. John C. Hadden. Lainie Hadden was president of the Junior League of Cleveland in 1971–72, and she immediately took a liking to Shepardson and his vision of saving the theaters at Playhouse Square. Lainie was bubbly and determined and used her position to champion not only Playhouse Square but also other causes throughout Cleveland. She had attended Laurel School and was student president at Vassar College, her alma mater. She was famously quoted telling the Junior Leaguers: "Ladies, we sleep with some of the most powerful men in Cleveland, our husbands. Get them to pull out their checkbooks."

In 1972, the anxiety and urgency to protect and save the theaters took on greater consequence. In May of that year, the Millcap Corporation began taking out bids to demolish 1515 Euclid Avenue. The space holding the Ohio and State Theaters would be used for parking as a first step toward redevelopment. Shepardson recognized the urgency being thrust upon his efforts to revitalize and use the theaters once again.

It was amid the looming crisis that Lainie Hadden sought the checkbooks and influence of local leaders. She convinced the Junior League and its president at the time, Mrs. Kenneth Felderman, to provide a $25,000 grant in June to the Playhouse Square Association. The money was to be used to purchase the buildings or provide seed money for other funding streams. The help could not have come soon enough, as the wrecking cranes were taking up positions on Euclid Avenue.

Elaine Hadden and Ray Shepardson. Hadden was an early backer and supporter of Shepardson's efforts to reopen the Playhouse Square Theaters. *Cleveland Memory Project. Cleveland State University.*

As the Millcap Corporation sought to gain permission to cut the curb on Euclid Avenue in preparation to bring down the two theaters, Oliver Henkel argued that the curb-cut permit needed to be delayed. Oliver "Pudge" Henkel was a lawyer at the Jones Day law firm in Cleveland. Shepardson credits Henkel's involvement as pivotal in saving the State and Ohio Theaters.

Henkel grew up in Mansfield and came to Cleveland by way of Yale University in 1964. He became involved in saving the theaters and restoring Playhouse Square through his efforts to delay the curb cut and remained active in Playhouse Square thereafter. In 1972, Henkel was the lawyer for the Junior League and through his connection with Lainie Hadden got involved in representing Playhouse Square and the Junior League at the hearing before Cleveland City Council and the Fine Arts Council. He was

successful and obtained a thirty-day delay in a decision as to whether a curb-cut permit would be granted.

During the delay, Henkel was able to negotiate a five-year lease for the Loew's buildings from Millcap Corporation. Playhouse Square Association now had control of both the State and Ohio Theaters, and the focus moved from the Allen Theater toward the State and Ohio. The $50,000-a-year lease also meant that the association had to start attracting many more people downtown. Henkel continued his involvement out of civic duty but also because Cleveland needed to improve its image. Jones Day was trying to recruit top-tier lawyers, and Cleveland needed an image boost for the firm to be successful. In 1973, Playhouse Square Association became Playhouse Square Foundation, and Oliver Henkel became the first president/chair of the foundation's board of trustees in August.

Opposite: Sign outside of Loew's State Theater coming down in preparation to tear down the theater to make space for a parking garage. Cleveland Press *photographer, Bill Nehez. Cleveland Memory Project. Cleveland State University.*

Above: Oliver Henkel (*right*) and his wife, Sally. Henkel was the first president of the Playhouse Square Association and instrumental in keeping the theaters from being torn down. *Cleveland Memory Project. Cleveland State University.*

Throughout the remainder of 1972, Playhouse Square Association put on a series of shows at the Allen Theater to generate patrons and build a cash-flow stream to pay the rent on the Loew's buildings. A total of eighteen concerts and performances were put on, in large part collaborating with Belkin Productions. At the same time, work began in earnest to clean up and ready the State Theater and protect the Ohio Theater.

Shepardson's volunteer crew expanded, and with Lainie Hadden convincing recruits to put some sweat equity into the theaters, the project gained steam. In an effort to keep an eye on the theaters, a number of spaces within the venues became home to both volunteers and paid staff. There was not much money available to pay the staff, so individuals like Ralph Smith, Chuck Fleming and Weldon Carpenter took up residence in the theaters. Spaces were carved out of former manager offices or the mezzanine men's room in the State to provide lodging. Countless hours were spent scraping paint, rewiring and generally cleaning up the theaters. The energy was the start of a volunteer tradition that continues today at Playhouse Square.

In the spring of 1973, Ray stopped in to see a production at Cleveland State University being put on by Joe Garry. The show was *Jacques Brel Is Alive and Well and Living in Paris*. It is a story put to music about Jacques Brel, a Belgian singer and songwriter. *Brel* had a successful run at Berea Summer Theater in 1972, and Joe Garry brought it downtown to Cleveland State's Factory Theater for a brief run in the spring of 1973.

The legend is that Shepardson was at a performance at the Factory Theater and asked whether Garry would be willing to stage the show at Playhouse Square's Cabaret Theater. Garry remarked that he didn't know that Playhouse Square had a cabaret. Ray said, "We will." During the walk-through at the State, Ray described where the stage would be constructed, where patrons would sit, how they would be fed and where they would enter. All of this description took place in an empty lobby.

Now the work pace quickened at the State. Floors needed to cleaned and polished. A stage had to be built, ticket prices set and tickets sold. A caterer had to be hired, and more volunteers would be needed to usher, bus tables and clean up after the shows. The frenzied work included hoisting chandeliers acquired from the Home Piano Center that at one time lit up the Commodore Perry Hotel in Toledo. The marble baseboards had eight layers of paint that had to be removed. The stage was constructed from salvaged framing used to hold up the Cinerama screen in the Ohio Theater. Five hundred yards of carpeting were purchased to cover the lobby floor, and chairs came from the Old Black Angus Restaurant.

Left to right: David O. Frazier, Theresa Piteo, Providence Hollander and Cliff Bemis, the actors in *Jacques Brel Is Alive and Well and Living in Paris*. *Cleveland Memory Project. Cleveland State University*.

Ralph "Smitty" Smith was so tired working double and triple hours on the lobby that he literally fell asleep on a ladder as the show was about to begin. But begin it did on April 18, 1973. It was scheduled to run three weeks as a trial run to see if patrons would come downtown to the theater. It was a smash hit, and the run was immediately extended from three weeks to six months. The cast of Providence Hollander, Theresa Piteo, Cliff Bemis and David O. Frazier performed the twenty-five songs about life and love to perfection, and the city fell in love with *Jacques Brel*.

Amazing as the success of the show was, it was equally amazing that the entire production was put together for only $35,000. The army of volunteers who cleaned and readied the lobby, built the stage and performed bus duties and usher roles presented a first-class atmosphere. In the first eight weeks, the performance drew eight thousand persons to the cabaret. Shepardson's dream of opening up Playhouse Square was inching closer to reality.

In show business, success lasts only until the next production. *Brel* proved that Clevelanders would come back downtown. But the question remained: What next?

The first task was to open up another theater. The Palace Theater was in great disarray, but the Grand Hall Lobby was in reasonably good shape. Work was already underway cleaning up the lobby, because in May 1973, the Women's Board of Hiram House held a Las Vegas/Monte Carlo night in the lobby. The fundraiser pushed Shepardson and his crew to accelerate the cleaning and clearing out of the Palace even as *Brel* was beginning to generate momentum. The seats were pulled from the Palace auditorium, and the stage was cleaned and prepared for guests, again largely through the hard work and efforts of volunteers.

The Palace next hosted the production of *Ben Bagley's Decline and Fall of the Entire World as Seen through the Eyes of Cole Porter.* The show provided a dinner and cocktail option in the Palace auditorium and stage, then moved to the Grand Hall lobby to watch the production. *The Decline and Fall,* directed by Joe Garry, was the second successful show produced locally by Playhouse Square. *Decline and Fall* opened in November 1973 and lasted until the start of summer 1974. The closing was due more to a lack of air-conditioning in the Palace than a drop in interest.

The second task was to expand the paid staff now that some money was coming into Playhouse Square. In 1973, Shepardson hired two young individuals who would make their mark on Playhouse Square. The first was a writer and recent graduate of Cleveland State University; the second was a man Ray had met over coffee and offered a salary derived from the coat-check room receipts.

Kathleen Kennedy was an English major at Cleveland State and, like so many of the admirers and followers of Ray and Playhouse Square, a Clevelander. In 1972, she was working on a master's degree in English and wrote a critically acclaimed adaptation of Dante's *Inferno.* Shepardson hired her as the public relations director for the Playhouse Square Foundation in the fall of 1973.

Kennedy worked hard despite a warning by her physician that she should take things easier due to a bronchial asthma condition she had from birth. In 1975, she published a book, *Playhouse Square,* that is affectionately identified as the "Redbook." In it, she describes the early history of Playhouse Square and theater in Cleveland. It is full of historical stories of who's who in Cleveland theater prior to the opening of the Playhouse Square theaters, complete with many pictures of what the theaters were like in the past and what they looked like as Playhouse Square was opening up again.

She was also the author of one of the productions presented by Playhouse Square in 1975, *Conversations with an Irish Rascal*. It was a great success and moved on to play Off-Broadway and in other cities across the country. Kathleen died unexpectedly in July 1975, just after the opening of *Conversations*. She was found in her apartment by close friends. Playhouse Square opened up Kennedy's, a small theater space under the lobby of the Ohio, several years later as a tribute to Kathleen. Kennedy's is still in use.

The second hire was John Hemsath, also a Clevelander. Hemsath had recently quit his job in New York City and returned to Cleveland. The news of the potential demolishing of the theaters and the work Shepardson was doing to help save them drew his interest. A mutual friend introduced Ray to John, and the two had a conversation over coffee at Swingos on Eighteenth and Euclid. A job was offered to Hemsath on the spot, and he accepted, thinking that it might be a "cool" job to have for a couple of years. It lasted thirty-eight years.

Shepardson did not have a great deal of money to offer Hemsath. *Brel* was still going strong in the State Cabaret, but Ray's offer for compensation was a $150 guarantee per week from the coat-check concession. During the day, Hemsath volunteered, as did many other Playhouse Square advocates. At night, he worked the coat check for *The Decline and Fall of the Entire World as Seen through the Eyes of Cole Porter*. In time, Hemsath started up the group sales office; shortly after that, special events director was added to his job list. He eventually became Shepardson's second in command.

Hemsath recognized right away that much of the theater space was in a sorry state of decay and neglect. The stages and backstage areas were unusable. The Ohio Theater was completely useless, with a warped auditorium floor and a fallen ceiling. All the theaters had ceiling damage. Often during *The Decline and Fall*, the lobby of the Palace had to be cleaned of plaster that had fallen from the ceiling overnight. Bus pans were set out in the attics of the theaters to catch dripping rain.

In 1972, Nick Spontelli wandered through the theaters after seeing a news story about the activities there. Nick had worked for Loew's as a stationary engineer starting in 1927. In 1968, when the theaters closed, he retired. In those early hectic days of readying the State Theater for performances, he was a great help. He knew the buildings. He knew the steam lines and water lines and taught Ralph Smith how to get the heating system up and running. Spontelli was a short guy but very strong, and he physically carried hundreds of pounds of roof tar to the top of the State Theater in buckets. He was able to get the large air-circulating fan in the State operational. Nick was one of those volunteers who provided an invaluable service as he helped get the theaters into some semblance of working order.

A small crew of three or four painters worked in the State auditorium while an audience was in the cabaret. Volunteer ushers held out straw hats at the end of performances to collect renovation money. Money was a constant need, and convincing people to come downtown, even for a great show like *Brel* or, later, *Conversations*, was a continuing issue. Once downtown, people had no place to go before or after the show, as most of the restaurants were closed around Playhouse Square.

Oliver Henkel also recognized the need to enhance the areas around Playhouse Square. A master plan was needed to create a neighborhood near the theaters. It was recognized that the theaters could not exist as islands. Within a short time, a connected part of the Playhouse Square Foundation umbrella was created: Playhouse Square Associates. The entity was designed to be a financial, development, investment and realty arm of the foundation. This aspect of the foundation was in keeping with a goal to utilize public-private partnerships to move projects linked to Playhouse Square forward in a quiet and professional manner. A Playhouse Square Advisory Board was also created to provide business and professional advice and assistance.

By 1976, the background work of the Playhouse Square organization was beginning to pay off. A $1 million loan was being evaluated to purchase the Loew's buildings, and a deal with the Spaghetti Factory restaurants and Cleveland State University was being explored. Playhouse Square was facing a $475,000 payment option on purchasing the Loew's Building. It was at that time that the Cleveland Foundation provided a $20,000 grant for hiring an executive director. The grant landed Gordon Bell. Bell was working in Washington State, where he was in charge of planning for Kitsap County. Bell and Shepardson were acquainted with each other from the Seattle area. The Cleveland Foundation support would prove to be the right boost at the right time for Playhouse Square.

Under Bell's guidance and with the unqualified support of the Cuyahoga County commissioners, Cuyahoga County purchased the Loew's Building for $681,000 (a lifeline once the loan and restaurant deals fell through).

Mr. and Mrs. Gordon Bell. Gordon Bell (*right*) was hired by the Playhouse Square
Foundation to bring additional business acumen to work with foundations and businesses.
Cleveland Memory Project. Cleveland State University.

Under the terms of the deal, the county would put $175,000 of initial improvements into the building for use as part of the juvenile court system. The court system would reside in offices where once the Stage Door Canteen and Cleveland Recording Company had been located. The county then leased back to the Playhouse Square Foundation the State and Ohio Theaters for twenty years. The first real protections for the theaters were now in place.

The tenuousness of Playhouse Square did not abate with the purchase of the Loew's Building. There was still the issue of the Palace and the Allen. Early in 1977, Shepardson and Bell had to consider whether the work on the Palace could continue, and the Allen Theater was an entirely other question. In June 1977, Playhouse Square determined that the focus should be on the State and Ohio and that the Palace Theater efforts should be abandoned. However, later that year, Bell negotiated a twenty-five-year lease for the Palace Theater, with plans for Playhouse Square to move the headliner performances from the State to the Palace. Playhouse Square turned away from the Allen Theater. A different production company created *Laserium*, a musical light show that lasted a few months at the Allen.

The purchase of the Loew's Building by the county allowed the Playhouse Square Foundation to seek funding streams from outside organizations. The Cleveland Foundation, seeing stability in the physical structure, provided another seed grant that was used to gain a Federal Economic Development grant of $3.1 million with the support of the City of Cleveland. The money was earmarked for new heating, plumbing, air-conditioning, roof work, seating and restoration of interior artwork. Another grant of $3.3 million was turned down. The second grant required the money to be used to convert the Ohio Theater into a conference center. Playhouse Square was committed to restoring the Ohio and State Theaters as theaters.

The foundation board hired Peter van Dijk to develop a plan for the Playhouse Square area in keeping with Oliver Henkel's thoughts that the theaters should not be islands but a neighborhood community. Van Dijk initially proposed a conceptual model surrounding a master plan for redevelopment of Playhouse Square. The plan called for downtown housing in and around the square, public areas, restaurants, retail shops and a hotel. The timeline for the master plan was between ten and twenty years, and by 1979, Playhouse Square Associates had purchased the Huron Point Building and supported retail and restaurants in the area, including a restaurant called the Rusty Scupper.

Late in 1977, Shepardson was fielding offers from other cities to do the same work at classic theaters that he was beginning to accomplish in Cleveland. An offer for the Playhouse Square Foundation to work on the Palace in Columbus and the Fountain Square RKO Palace in Cincinnati was presented to Shepardson. Both offers arrived with the work still not completed in Cleveland. Ray was excited about the prospects of taking his vision for old theaters on the road. Playhouse Square's board was not as thrilled. Beginning in 1978, Shepardson and Playhouse Square began to move in different directions. Henkel was just setting up a line of credit for the foundation to book big-name acts, and in 1977–78, close to five hundred thousand people attended shows at the Playhouse Square Center.

Shepardson did in fact act as a consultant overseeing the work in Cincinnati and was extremely impressed with the amount of business and community support for restoring the Fountain Square Palace. He commented that it took Cincinnati eleven months to do what Cleveland was working on for eight years. John Lewis, a Cleveland partner in the law firm Squires, Sanders, and Dempsey, succeeded Henkel at Playhouse Square Foundation. He reflected the growing attitude that Shepardson and Cleveland were moving in different directions.

Late in 1979, Shepardson was granted permission to work in other cities (St. Louis, Louisville and Columbus) as a consultant. He and his wife started Playhouse Management as a consulting firm. By the end of 1979, he had left, with a number of disparaging comments about the negative atmosphere in Cleveland and the planning at Playhouse Square.

Shepardson left Cleveland but did not leave theater restoration. Over the next twenty years, Ray lived in multiple cities simultaneously and was instrumental in more than forty restorations of historic theaters across the country. Included in that list is the Palace Theater in Louisville, Kentucky; the Palace Theater in Cincinnati, Ohio; the Fox Theater in Detroit, Michigan; and the Chicago Theater in Chicago, Illinois. His time in Cleveland was not done; he returned in the 1990s to save one more theater and as a result create the opportunity for expansion of Playhouse Square.

LAWRENCE WILKER—RENOVATOR

John Lewis believed that Ray Shepardson was the father of the Playhouse Square miracle. However, as a visionary, Ray did not deal with the business community or foundations as well as he should have. Lewis believed that for Playhouse Square to go to the next level, a different leader was needed. Experience in theater and the business of working with philanthropic organizations was a must. At first, Lewis turned to Charles Raison.

Raison was a college teacher, chair of the theater department at Lycoming College in Williamsport, Pennsylvania. He was appointed executive director of Dramatic Arts in New York City, where he developed a West Coast branch of the academy and opened a theater in Pasadena, California. He oversaw renovation projects in Virginia City, Nevada, and Lancaster, New York. Just prior to coming to Cleveland, he was the director of planning and development for the Studio Arena Theater in Buffalo. He turned a burlesque theater into a 630-seat legitimate theater. Charles replaced Gordon Bell and then took over for Shepardson when he left in 1979.

Playhouse Square was gaining momentum, and under Raison several key and influential grants were obtained. In 1980, a $710,000 Cleveland Foundation grant was obtained to support renovation and operating funds. The grant was designed as a challenge grant to jump-start Playhouse Square in the search for $18 million to renovate and ready the State Theater. The renovation work and capital campaign were aimed at satisfying the Cleveland Ballet and Cleveland Opera Company in setting up residence at Playhouse Square.

Playhouse Square early in 1980 started a "last chance" capital improvement plan, with the business model being the operation of the State, Palace and Ohio Theaters as an entertainment center. The ambitious fundraising plan called for a combination of federal grants, county grants, city support and private community donations. Under Raison, the idea of Playhouse Square Center began to take shape and large-scale renovations to the State and Ohio Theaters were planned.

The foundation was unsure which theater to renovate. It initially planned to work on the State Theater. George Voinovich was sure. Voinovich, the mayor of Cleveland, fondly remembers being at the theaters when he was courting his wife. He was a strong supporter of the project, first as a county commissioner and then as mayor. Great Lakes Shakespeare Festival was contemplating a move from Lakewood and looking for a new home. One consideration was building a new space near the lakefront in downtown Cleveland. Mayor Voinovich insisted that any move be not to a new space, rather it should be to Playhouse Square. His push for the festival to move into Playhouse Square Center was the deciding factor regarding which theater to renovate. The Ohio Theater was perfect in size for the Shakespearian company and would be the focal point for renovation.

Raison did not remain in Cleveland to see his plans completed, as he left in 1982, just as work on the theater renovations was moving forward. He came into Cleveland being considered a "master builder" of theaters and left with a building momentum and a funding momentum to carry the projects forward. In his place, the Playhouse Square Foundation board brought in Lawrence Wilker.

Wilker was actually recruited by a headhunter for the position. He was working for the Schubert organization as director of properties (both theaters and real estate) in charge of twenty-three theaters in New York and across the country. He came to Cleveland with an academic background in theater, with a degree in economics, an MFA in theater and a PhD in theater. His first renovation project was the Grand Opera House in Wilmington, Delaware, a $70 million project to fully restore the venue to its original 1871 glory. As the new president of Playhouse Square, he found himself with multiple challenges. He had many hats, being in charge of theater renovation, financial development, theater productions and subscriptions, and he was in some part working with Playhouse Square Associates to acquire and develop real estate, in keeping with the master plan to create a neighborhood. During Wilker's nine years at Playhouse Square, the theaters and the foundation gained stability and created the third-largest theater center in the country.

John Hemsath was still working at Playhouse Square and was promoted to director of theater operations. He remembers Wilker being a terrific boss. Wilker's experience and understanding of the business of theaters put Playhouse Square on a sound footing. Where Shepardson would use ticket money as cash flow, Wilker placed the money in escrow. Shepardson's actions almost created a huge issue when ticket sales to a concert by Cher were spent as operating funds. When the show was canceled, the money, which was no longer there, had to be refunded.

Wilker's first job was overseeing completion of the renovations on the Ohio Theater. The Ohio had been in very poor shape. The walls in the auditorium were painted red. Plaster was falling down, and the floor suffered from extreme water damage. There were no seats, and some of the theater had been scavenged to support early fix-up work in the lobby of the State. Early in the process, it was determined that as much of the Ohio's original design as possible should be preserved.

With that goal in mind, Peter van Dijk used a palette of green and ivory, allowing the auditorium to have a cool and understated look. The ceiling

The Ohio Theater undergoing renovations during the 1982 restoration project under Larry Wilker. *Cleveland Memory Project. Cleveland State University.*

with its plaster medallions was restored, but the detail on the plaster figures was skipped due to budget constraints. A chandelier from the Hippodrome Theater was hung in the dome, and green seats matching the stage curtains were set. The reconstituted auditorium had a new rake to improve sight lines and ended up having a 1,035-seat capacity, slightly smaller than the original 1,338 seats.

The stage could not be enlarged, with the wings being shallow and the total number of rigging lines capped at fifty-one. Nonetheless, the forty-by-forty-foot stage and twenty-six-foot proscenium opening provided a generous look, and the stage had a number of traps. The dressing rooms were smaller but functional, and other than cleaning up, they were not changed. There was a decision to limit workshop and storage space under the stage due to finances and the rush to complete the theater in time.

The lobby, once a masterpiece, became simply functional. The length of the original lobby was kept intact, but the carpeting and infinity mirror side walls provided a temporary look. Overall, the lobby presented an art deco mix with contemporary design.

The real excitement was in opening the venue as a legitimate theatrical space for the first time since 1933. Vincent Dowling, the artistic director of Great Lakes Shakespeare Festival, was overjoyed and looking forward to taking up residence in the newly restored Ohio. The first performance was *As You Like It* in July 1982. The opening of the Ohio was the first step toward re-creating Playhouse Square.

The work on Playhouse Square was moving forward on many levels. Larry Wilker first put on his performance directors' hat. Planning and booking events was also an early priority. The first year of operation at the Ohio saw a wide variety of performances. In addition to Great Lakes Shakespeare Festival, which included *As You Like It, The Playboy of the Western World* and the first North American presentation of *Life and Adventures of Nicholas Nickleby*, the schedule saw jazz performances, the Cleveland Opera, the Ohio Chamber Orchestra, Ohio Ballet and the first of many return visits by Pilobolus for the Cleveland Modern Dance Association. In keeping with outreach and educational goals, Wilker put on the first Children's Theatre Series in cooperation with the Junior League of Cleveland.

The next hat Wilker had to put on was that of employer. The large number of tasks and the variety of connections needed to continue progress could not be accomplished by one person. As previously indicated, Wilker promoted John Hemsath to director of theater operations. Over the next few years, Wilker added Art Falco, Tom Einhouse and Gina Vernaci to the Playhouse Square staff. They all remained with the foundation and played important roles as Playhouse Square grew into its master plan. Falco became president of Playhouse Square Foundation, and Vernaci would follow him into that position. Einhouse become vice-president of facilities and capital and was later a driving force behind property acquisition and theater renovation. Additionally, Wilker put in place the organizational structure that kept the foundation moving forward and provided continuity into the future.

The Ohio Theater renovation was completed, but the pressure to move forward was still present. The next task and next deadline would be renovating the State Theater. In order for Cleveland Ballet to set up residence at the State, a new stage and stagehouse were needed. Building a new stagehouse required the purchase of additional property and a $7 million commitment of funds. Work on fundraising had to continue, and work on construction had to proceed.

Playhouse Square continued to work with public and private partners to achieve goals. Cuyahoga County commissioners pitched in by using eminent domain powers to acquire property behind the State Theater on East Seventeenth Street toward Chester Avenue. A court battle ensued, but the county prevailed, and land was used to expand the stage of the State Theater. The $7 million stage project and refurbishment of the State auditorium was completed in June 1984, just in time to host the Metropolitan Opera.

The new stagehouse at the State was one of the finest in the country. The stage size was expanded enough to place a full basketball court on it. Behind the stage was a loading dock and storage area to hold props and equipment for any sized show. Also, behind the stage were first-class dressing rooms, and above the backstage area were practice rooms, complete with dance bars and mirrors. Under the stage were additional dressing areas, storage and an orchestra pit large enough to hold eighty musicians.

The auditorium had new seats, chandeliers and audio equipment. The delicate plaster reliefs modeled after the Adams school were painstakingly restored. Terpsichore, the muse of choral song and dancing, looks down on the stage, beaming with pride equal to the meaning of her Greek name, "Delighting in Dance." The muse is an appropriate vision, as much of the stage and theater was reconstituted to suit Cleveland Ballet. The stage itself was specifically designed and constructed to allow a spring support, making it easier on the legs of dancers and performers.

The auditorium was set to seat 3,100 patrons. The marble banisters around the back of the stage and on the steps leading to the mezzanine and balcony areas were polished and restored to the original glory of 1921. New carpeting was placed throughout, and the lobby was set to an original look with the removal of the changes that were put in place when the State was a cabaret for *Jacques Brel*.

Opening night for the State was a multiday affair mimicking the celebration when the State opened anew. A dinner pavilion area was set up in Palace Theater for first-night ticketholders. Invited guests from across the country were present, and the opening performance by the Metropolitan Opera was *Peter Grimes*. It is the story of a man who returns from the dead; the same story that was part of the original 1921 opening night for Playhouse Square's other open theater, the Ohio.

The opening of the State was a total success, and momentum was gaining for creating Playhouse Square Center. Lawrence Wilker's work was still not complete. While the State was opening to toasts across the city, another fundraising effort was being planned by Wilker and the foundation board under John Lewis. The State was opened, but money was still needed to begin work on the Palace Theater.

Wilker had to put on his development director hat with little time to take bows. Dates and performers had to be booked for the Ohio and State Theaters. Playhouse Square now had over four thousand seats to keep filled. His life was still very busy, and the success of Playhouse Square was not guaranteed. A new computerized ticketing service was put into place to make it more reliable and easier to make ticket reservations and purchases. There was still a need for several million dollars to be raised for work on the restoration of the Palace.

Work on restoring the Palace Theater began in earnest soon after the opening of the State Theater. The venue was without seats, and as was true with the other venues, much of the ornate ceiling work had to be restored. The cost was $8.2 million, and the actual work lasted almost two years. Begun in 1987, the job was completed in the spring of 1988. The grand reopening featured Burt Bacharach and Dionne Warwick in a concert attended by 2,200 patrons who paid up to $350. Tables were sold to corporate donors for $10,000. The glitz and glamor of the 1920s was back, and the city fell in love with the Palace once again. The marble, chandeliers, polished brass railings and the Sevres Blue Vase were on display, helping to recapture the ambiance of the original 1922 opening night for the "finest theater in the world."

All seemed well for Playhouse Square, and with the restoration and opening of three grand theaters, the future looked bright. However, the story of Playhouse Square, like many other great dramas, was not a simple one, even after a success like the reopening of the Palace. Down the street a short way was the Bulkley Building and the abandoned Allen Theater. The State, Ohio and Palace had been saved from the wrecking ball and restored, but the scene was about to be replayed for the Allen. The new owner of the Bulkley complex, William West, had plans to demolish the Allen and create an urban courtyard and shopping complex. West bought the complex from the Cleveland Foundation in 1987. A sense of urgency was growing: Could the last of Euclid's grand theaters be saved? In two years, the "Save the Allen" group was unable to obtain a developer willing to take on the task of refurbishing the venue. In 1990, the planned urban courtyard was changed to a landscaped, two-level parking garage. A sense of déjà vu was settling in at Playhouse Square. Larry Wilker explored either renting or buying the Allen, but the rent scale and asking price by West was out of reach for the foundation, already involved in other realty operations and projects. Unfortunately, the Allen Theater would have to wait until after Wilker left Playhouse Square in 1991.

Allen Theater marquee. The Allen Theater was threatened with demolition after three other theaters at Playhouse Square were already open. *Cleveland Memory Project. Cleveland State University.*

Wilker and Playhouse Square juggled many projects at the same time. The long-term master plan of creating a neighborhood about the square was a continuing project that had been around when Wilker arrived. In the midst of saving and restoring three theaters at a cost of $37 million, the master plan moved forward. Wilker also believed that the theaters could not live as islands on their own, just as Oliver Henkel had thought. Playhouse Square Development Corporation, with help from foundations and private individuals, quietly began purchasing property around the square.

First, Playhouse Square Associates brought in the Rusty Scupper chain after acquiring the former Black Angus Restaurant. The Associates, the investment arm of Playhouse Square Foundation, spent close to $1 million refurbishing the space. Next was the acquisition of the Huron Pointe Building in front of the Halle Building. Playhouse Square Associates put together the money to purchase the building and then eventually turned it over to the Development Corporation. The Cleveland Foundation purchased the Lake/Esquire/WJW TV building and the Bulkley Building. The Bulkley was sold to West and Associates, but the old Esquire movie house was torn down and the land given to Playhouse Square.

In 1987, the foundation, with the support of the City of Cleveland, purchased land behind the Bulkley Building to construct a parking garage to provide parking for theatergoers and to provide a stream of cash to help offset the operation of the theaters. Planning also began that year on utilizing property owned under the Playhouse Square Development Corporation at Huron Point and on East Fourteenth Street. Those plans came to fruition starting in 1988 with a new office building on land that once hosted the Rusty Scupper on East Fourteenth Street, along with a parking garage, and the foundation was seeking a developer for a hotel on Huron Point. Playhouse Square was able to build and then sell the Renaissance office building it constructed and start a small endowment fund using the profits from the sale.

One other action that Wilker supervised during the 1980s was the purchase of the booking agency that brought Broadway shows to Cleveland. The gentleman who had operated and controlled touring shows coming to Cleveland was retiring, and Wilker put up a sizable amount of cash to acquire the business. It was one more risk in a long line of risks that Playhouse Square Foundation under Wilker's leadership took that eventually paid off brilliantly. Unfortunately, moving Broadway road shows to the Palace Theater spelled doom for the Hanna. Without the subscriber base and the influx of traveling Broadway shows, the Hanna closed in 1989.

Wilker's success at Playhouse Square garnered national attention. In 1991, he was offered the opportunity to take over the Kennedy Center in Washington, D.C. The challenge of overcoming a $2 million deficit and an infrastructure that was coming apart in a highly visible national setting was one that he ultimately could not refuse. Wilker found great success revitalizing the Kennedy Center, just as he had in setting Playhouse Square on the right path during his nine years as president. He left the foundation on solid ground, with three fully restored theaters, property interests through the square, a growing Broadway subscription series and annual attendance of over 750,000 patrons.

Playhouse Square Foundation still had some loose ends to finish with Wilker's departure. Among the issues were finding a developer for the proposed hotel, what to do to protect the Allen Theater and, after 1989, what to do about the Hanna Theater. Finally, who would take over the reins of Playhouse Square Foundation and protect the gains made and expand into the future?

Art Falco—Growth and Development

Art Falco was hired by Larry Wilker in 1985 as chief financial officer after having worked for the Diamond Shamrock Corporation. A Cleveland native, Falco was named vice-president for finance and administration to Playhouse Square Foundation in 1988. He was selected to succeed Wilker from fifty-one other applicants in a national search.

When hired, Falco indicated that his top priorities would be to continue Playhouse Square's excellence in presenting first-class entertainment of all varieties. The variety included the six resident companies (Cleveland Ballet, Cleveland Opera, Dance Cleveland, the renamed Great Lakes Theater Festival, Ohio Ballet and support of Cuyahoga Community College's arts program) and the Broadway series, jazz events, music concerts and ethnic ensembles. Playhouse Square's something-for-everyone approach would be a continuing goal under his leadership.

Programming would not be his first challenge; that would be dealing with the lingering problem regarding the Allen. Since 1988, the owners of the Allen Theater and Bulkley Building wavered between selling the Bulkley and Allen or demolishing it to create a shopping area complete with an open-air courtyard. Playhouse Square Foundation offered to purchase the building, but William West and Associates set the price higher than the foundation was willing to pay, especially since other property ventures were in play.

The Allen received several reprieves, first from the Landmark Commission in 1988–89 and then from the Fine Arts Commission in 1990. All of the delays were aimed at trying to find some way to save the theater. In 1991, the City Planning Commission agreed to a plan that would retain the ornate rotundas in the Allen and reuse parts for a restaurant. A lack of tenant interest or other development ideas pushed West to consider demolishing the entire theater. The push was delayed again while the City Planning Commission reorganized due to the addition of new members. It was in 1993 when Falco and Playhouse Square Foundation were able to reach a lease agreement with West. William West was facing mortgage payment issues with no new tenants and a $6 million purchase agreement since 1987. Those factors, plus a willingness on the part of Falco and the foundation to cover the cost to improvements in the lease agreement, finally carried the day.

With the Allen Theater now under control, Falco could turn his attention to programming for the current operating theaters and the soon-to-be-used Allen Theater. It took a year to ready the Allen for a performance, but in November 1994, Falco and Playhouse Square turned once again to the magic of a cabaret. *Forever Plaid* was produced by Playhouse Square in a functionally renovated Allen auditorium. The theater was cleaned (mostly by volunteers), the bathrooms were modernized and heating and ventilation systems were updated. The final seating reconfiguration was 350, using tables and chairs placed in a raked seating arrangement around a small stage. The seating capacity was a far cry from the 3,000-plus the original Allen had when it opened in 1921. The theater was not fully restored, allowing patrons to catch glimpses of past glory and imagine what a completely restored Allen might look like.

Falco was not going to rest on his laurels in providing quality and varied entertainment to Playhouse Square. The addition of the Allen Theater allowed the foundation to make the run toward being the second-largest operating theater arts center outside of Lincoln Center in New York. In 1993, Falco negotiated a merger with Cleveland's Front Row Theater. The Front Row was originally built in 1974 in Highland Heights. The theater had a capacity of 3,200 people spaced around a circular stage that revolved, allowing patrons to have a clear view of the performances. Seats in the last row were only fifty-nine feet from the stage. The focus was on Las Vegas–style entertainment, with headliners such as Sammy Davis Jr. and Wayne Newton. The move downtown to Playhouse Square brought the bookings into the Playhouse Square Center.

In 1995, Falco oversaw the next phase of Playhouse Square's development with the opening of the $27 million Wyndham Hotel at Huron Point. Since 1989, Playhouse Square had worked with a number of different developers to build a hotel in front of the Halle Building. There were a number of starts and stops in garnering the finances to get the project off the ground. Finally, in 1994, the money and the developer were found to begin the hotel, and in 1995, the Wyndham opened.

Playhouse Square Foundation was always looking for ways to collect financial support. The grand opening of the Wyndham was one more way to sustain itself. The opening delivered more than $200,000 from partygoers who attended and were entertained with the music of Cole Porter, Irving Berlin and Rodgers and Hammerstein. The patrons then enjoyed oysters on the half shell at the Windsor Restaurant, all preceding a dinner on the State Theater stage. Dancing followed, then more music in the State lobby, the Ohio lobby and at Kennedy's.

The completion of the hotel at Playhouse Square focused Art Falco's attention on what might be accomplished entertainment-wise if the

Allen Theater could be completely restored. *Forever Plaid* and then *Shear Madness* had successful runs in the Allen cabaret, but in order to have long-run Broadway shows, more space was needed. The Allen provided an option for growth. With that goal in mind, Playhouse Square Foundation opened another round of fundraising, seeking an additional $15 million in investment from primarily private donations. The money would be used to completely restore the Allen Theater, including a new stagehouse. Playhouse Square had already shown success in its past efforts, and obtaining the money seemed a sure bet.

The bet paid off because, in September 1997, Cleveland mayor Mike White and County Commissioners Jane Campbell, Tim Hagen and Tim McCormack put on their hard hats and watched as the wrecking ball began tumbling the back wall of the Allen Theater's eight-story stagehouse. This time, the wrecking ball was embraced, as the new stagehouse would create space for Broadway shows to open extended stays in Cleveland. At the time, Art Falco indicated that using the Allen Theater for extended Broadway performances would draw 500,000 people to Playhouse Center and add $30 million to the local economy—a nice return for a $15 million investment.

The new stagehouse expanded the overall size of the stage to 110 feet wide and 116 feet deep and added dressing rooms and storage underneath. The renovation also cleaned and restored the ornamental plaster and revealed four paintings at the front of the ceiling. The paintings had been painted over, and the restoration process was able to uncover them and bring them back to their former elegance. One of those paintings was named *The Lady of the Allen Theater* and resides in the ceiling overlooking the auditorium and just above the proscenium. Grillwork was gilded and glazed, and the six faux windows and the balustraded balconies were completely restored with backlighting to create atmospheric lighting, as was present in 1921.

The opening night was once again a great celebration. Euclid Avenue was blocked off with a temporary stage set up for dignitaries. The theater was set to have 2,500 patrons, bringing the total number of seats at Playhouse Square to 9,500, solidifying Cleveland's claims to the second-largest theater complex in the United States. Burgundy drapes hid the restored marquee; with fireworks, the marquee was unveiled. The VIP crowd entered the newly restored theater and got their first looks at the lobby rotunda and reconstituted auditorium. The opening performance was *Jolson: The Musical*.

Things were looking up for Playhouse Square. However, one more performance space was missing from the final act. Across the street on Fourteenth, the Hanna Theater had been closed since 1989. In 1993, Ray Shepardson returned to Cleveland in an attempt to reopen it. His task was to raise $3 million to convert the Hanna from a traditional theater into a cabaret. He would remove the seats on the main floor and install three terraces, allowing tables to be set up. The changes were made in a way to protect the original theater design, allowing things to be changed back if the need arises. It took two years to raise a third of the money.

This time around, Shepardson was not trying to create a nonprofit corporation but rather a for-profit commercial venture. His plans were big. He hoped to be able to stage nineteen shows a week at the Hanna using a double-booking process and placing shows in repertory. He would also have a children's matinee and a Saturday night "jam session" after midnight. Besides looking for success once again with a cabaret, he contracted with Joe Garry to work on developing the children's shows. He also found Elaine Hadden to be a principal shareholder in the enterprise. Shepardson was nothing if not ambitious.

Shepardson was able to open the Hanna in 1997 with a performance of *All Night Strut!* The show, which had its roots in Cleveland at a venue in the flats—Pickle Bills—was well liked in the city. He brought the show over to Playhouse Square in 1976. It was successful, and Cleveland audiences were receptive. The show lasted a few months and provided a good start for the newly designed Hanna. Two other shows played at the Hanna in the winter of 1998 (*Forbidden Broadway* and *A Brief History of White Music*), but neither drew big crowds despite the entertainment value of both. In the summer of 1998, Shepardson closed the Hanna for the summer, but the theater never opened again under his leadership. The problem was that being a for-profit venture was riskier and needed more financial backing than was available at that time. His successes restoring theaters and creating cabaret venues across the country helped jump-start the process with the Hanna, but past events could not sustain the future. Ray Shepardson left Cleveland for good that winter.

In 1999, an estate dispute within the Grogan family provided an opportunity for Art Falco to extend Playhouse Square's control of the square and move forward with long-term master plans. T.W. Grogan Company had held ownership of the Hanna Building, the Hanna Annex and the Hanna Theater since 1958. In 1991, the sons sued their father to take control of the company, and a new court battle ensued as a possible sale of the Hanna complex was being considered.

In August, the foundation purchased the Hanna properties for $17.5 million, along with two small parking lots and two small buildings between the Hanna and East Seventeenth Street. Falco's goal at the time was to reopen the Hanna Theater and remodel the Hanna buildings. The office buildings and annex would be turned into for-profit office space or perhaps apartments, inching closer to the foundation's long-term goal of creating a neighborhood and a twenty-four/seven area around the square.

In the late summer of 2000, Falco was able to bring another show into the Hanna Cabaret: *Tony 'n' Tina's Wedding*. The show opened to marvelous reviews, and the import from Minnesota appeared to be settling in for a long run, recapturing some of the cabaret magic that had long existed at Playhouse Square. In fact, the play ran for more than 800 performances, surpassing the *Jacques Brel* record of 522.

As *Tony 'n' Tina's Wedding* was being considered, another purchase opportunity opened up for Falco. In January 2000, Playhouse Square Foundation closed on a deal to buy the Bulkley Building, where the Allen Theater was located, as well as the foundation's offices. The addition of the Bulkley Building increased the real estate portfolio of the foundation to include the Loew's State and Ohio Theaters, the Hanna Building, Hanna Theater, development sites east of the Hanna on Euclid Avenue, the Wyndam Cleveland Hotel, a 750-car garage on Chester Avenue, a restaurant and the One Playhouse Square office building. Playhouse Square also had a 135-year lease on the Palace Theater, housed in the Keith Building. The neighborhood that Falco was looking to create around the theaters was close to complete.

Always looking for new opportunities, Falco created a Times Square look about Playhouse Square with the installation of video boards on the Hanna Building and the Wyndam Cleveland Hotel. The screens provide news tickers and promotions for events at Playhouse Square and around Cleveland. The net effect was to enhance the theater district atmosphere around the square. In 2002, he also made plans to renovate One Playhouse Square for $30 million. The newly remolded building became the home to WVIZ and WCPN (local public broadcasting radio and TV stations) in a partnership aimed at an expansion of educational programs at Playhouse Square. The unique partnership was the first in the country between a performing arts center and a public broadcasting organization. The remodel also provided another theater space for Playhouse Square, a three-hundred-seat black box–style theater that can be modified based on the needs of both the foundation and WVIZ/WCPN Ideastream and a dance rehearsal hall in the front of the building. Additionally, the changes provide a sneak peek behind the curtain of public broadcasting with the use of large windows framing a multimedia studio and the rehearsal hall. The changes also repurposed the six-story building erected in 1912 that once housed a furniture store and the headquarters of Stouffer Corporation, which operated a restaurant in the space for several decades. The costs for remodeling and operating the space were shared by both organizations.

Just as the Idea Center was opening up, Playhouse Square was having conversations with Great Lakes Theater Festival about the festival's desire to have a more intimate space and a thrust stage area. Falco was listening, and so was the director of programming at Playhouse Square, Gina Vernaci. Vernaci was looking for ways to free up performance space for smaller touring shows that prefer the one-thousand-seat Ohio to the larger State or Palace Theaters. The result of those conversations was a plan to re-imagine the Hanna Theater.

The Hanna was successfully being used as a cabaret-style theater, and the recent success of *Tony 'n' Tina's Wedding* and *Late Night Catechism* demonstrated interest by the Cleveland public in those types of shows. A newly reconstituted Great Lakes Theater Company needed a different space to meet the needs of its subscribers. How to accommodate both interest groups was the challenge. The Hanna would need to be remodeled again, and financial support would be required.

Great Lakes Theater Company and Playhouse Square went out into the foundation world and again used a public-private partnership approach to garner $19 million. The money was planned to be used to both renovate the Hanna and provide an endowment for the Great Lakes Theater Company. The Kresge Foundation contributed $1 million through a challenge grant once Great Lakes achieved $18 million, putting the fundraising effort over the top. It also helped that Tom Hanks, the one and only Forrest Gump, was one of the pitchmen for the campaign.

Hanks had been a member of Great Lakes Shakespeare Festival in 1977 when he started his career. The job with Great Lakes was his first, and he made forty-five dollars doing small parts in plays like *The Two Gentlemen of Verona* and *A Midsummer Night's Dream*. He regularly reflected on his time in Lakewood at Great Lakes and attributes much of his success to what he learned and put into practice while on stage working for Vincent Dowling, the creative director.

The re-imagined Hanna was downsized to an audience of 550 patrons with a large thrust stage complete with a hidden orchestra pit and a state-

The re-imagined Hanna Theater auditorium after renovations to prepare the space for Great Lakes Theater. *Author's photo, 2018.*

of-the-art audio system. The seating in the orchestra is comfortable, with excellent sight lines. The balcony had box seats and front-row mezzanine seating. Two historic boxes were renovated and provide an up-close overview of the stage area. The lower seating area had unique lounge seats—general admission seats presented in a comfortable sofa design, banquet seats and seats around a bar area near the back of the orchestra seating area. The bar was a gift of Tom Hanks. There is also a side room for before- or after-show gatherings.

The architectural ambiance of Sampietro's original work was protected, complete with coiffured ceiling and Italian Renaissance and Pompeian neoclassical plaster work. The small lobby area remained true to the original design and remained reminiscent of the lobbies one might find off of Forty-Second Street in New York. A ticket office and a gift shop are found just off the lobby, and the theater is accessible for those who have disabilities. The new theater opened for the fall season of 2008.

The Hanna was no sooner opened up for Great Lakes Theater than word came that the Cleveland Play House was about to lose its longtime home at East Eighty-Fifth Street between Euclid and Carnegie. The

Cleveland Play House is the longest-running professional theater in the United States, having been in continuous operation since 1915. Since 1926, the venue operated on land donated by prominent Cleveland industrialist Frances Drury where his Euclid Avenue mansion once stood. The moving force behind the purchase of the land was the Cleveland Clinic, which surrounded the property. The clinic gave Cleveland Play House an offer it couldn't refuse, as the venue had $1 million in facility maintenance costs and mounting debt.

The news regarding the Cleveland Play House provided yet another opportunity for Art Falco to strengthen Playhouse Square Center and merge a plan being discussed with Cleveland State University to create space at the downtown theater district. The space planned for this next merger would be the Allen Theater. Two years and $30 million later, the 2,500-seat Allen was transformed into an intimate, 500-plus-seat performance space, creating the "power of three" performance center.

The Power of Three is a collaboration among the Cleveland Play House, Cleveland State University and Playhouse Square Foundation. When Cleveland Play House entered the new setting, it brought with it its connection to Case Western Reserve University's graduate acting program. At the Allen, Case Western students work alongside professionals at the playhouse, and Cleveland State University undergraduates learn theater in a real-world setting. Playhouse Square Center cemented its place as the second-largest performing arts center in the United States (behind only Lincoln Center in New York), and with outreach into two universities and schools throughout northeast Ohio through Great Lakes and Cleveland Play House's student programs, established itself as a premier educational theater center as well. The collaboration created an entity larger than the sum of its parts.

The renovation of the Allen brought an economic synergy linking fundraising campaigns of the Cleveland Play House, Playhouse Square and Cleveland State University. The fundraising unity helped to overcome the market crash of 2008–9, allowing the Allen to be remodeled and two additional stages to be constructed. The Second Stage and the Lab Theater were built on space that was being used as parking lots. Falco brought Playhouse Square into a new era—where once parking lots were planned for old theaters, now new theaters were built where parking lots had existed.

There were a few more pieces of the puzzle to which Falco now turned his attention. He often referred to Playhouse Square as a twenty-four/

seven neighborhood. A neighborhood has boundaries and a uniqueness all its own. It also has shops and restaurants willing to cater to people living and working in the neighborhood.

The first step was creating living spaces. Playhouse Square sold the Hanna Annex, the building where the Hanna Theater was located, to a rental development specialist company. K&D properties bought the annex with the goal of creating apartments. Falco had long wanted to create living space around Playhouse Square, and K&D would make that happen. The sale included a long-term lease for the Hanna Theater.

Next was setting boundaries for the neighborhood. With that in mind, Playhouse Square Foundation constructed four gold-and-bronze gateway arches, creating entryways to the theater district on Euclid at East Thirteenth, Huron Road and East Fourteenth Street at Prospect. Designer Danny Barnycz included eight-foot-high digital kiosks decorated with gryphons like those found within the theaters and placed them throughout the boundaries of Playhouse Square. The final addition was the 8,500-pound GE outdoor chandelier—a dazzling exclamation mark for the district. The chandelier "defines Playhouse Square as a destination, which makes us unlike any performing arts center in the United States," according to Gina Vernaci.

Going back to the future, Falco and Playhouse Square began an ambitious $100 million fundraising effort titled Advancing the Legacy. The five-year campaign was focused on expenses, operation and an endowment. Once again, private donations from foundations and individuals advanced the goals of Playhouse Square, achieving and exceeding the target in 2019.

Finally, there was one more restoration project to be completed. The lobby of the Ohio Theater was only meant to be temporary when it opened in 1982. In 2015, Playhouse Square began an extensive research and renovation project to re-create the glamorous lobby that once dazzled the community. Under the direction of Tom Einhouse and in conjunction with EverGreene Architectural Arts, the Thomas Lamb palace in Italy was made new again. With the use of old photographs, written records and fragments of paint and plaster and original blueprints, the lobby was rebuilt. The final product was hailed as a triumph of craftsmanship and attention to detail. More than 8,500 hours of plaster sculpting and reproduction by master painters of three murals replicating the three lost in the 1964 fire resulted in a stunning restoration.

Tom Einhouse, the vice-president of facilities and capital for Playhouse Square, helped to oversee the restoration. He was part of the renovation

Restored Ohio Theater lobby in 2017 after a $3 million restoration to bring the lobby back to the glory of the 1920s. *Author's photo 2018.*

efforts at the foundation since the mid-1980s, when he was hired by Larry Wilker. He was very much Art Falco's right-hand man during the expansion and growth success during the 1990s and 2000s. He often does not get the credit that he deserves for his work behind the scenes. However, in the entrance to the Allen Theater, a cameo of Tom placed in the restored ceiling attests to the quiet impact he has on Playhouse Square. He is identified as a power player within Cleveland. The high-profile restoration of the Ohio lobby was a work of passion and pride, and its completion promoted Playhouse Square as the largest theater restoration project in the United States. As of this writing, Einhouse quietly oversees the commercial development side of Playhouse Square District Development Corporation's one-million-square-foot real estate portfolio as executive vice-president.

As Falco's tenure leading Playhouse Square's day-to-day operations ended in 2019, there was still the neighborhood aspect of the plan to complete. In 2018, the property that the foundation had acquired in 1999 with the acquisition of the Hanna was about to be used to enlarge his vision of a twenty-four/seven neighborhood. A three-hundred-plus-apartment, thirty-four-story building was erected across the street from the Conner Palace Theater. The project had a price tag of $135 million and is wholly owned by Playhouse Square's District Development Corporation. Along with the apartments, a 550-space parking garage was built to provide parking not only for the Lumen Building but also for patrons attending shows in the theater district.

Although his work is not finished at Playhouse Square, Art Falco established a lasting legacy that put the foundation on a solid footing. As the one-hundred-year anniversary approaches, Playhouse Square finds itself the second-largest performing arts center in the country, the largest theater renovation project in the country, the largest Broadway Series subscription base in the country and a destination center for visitors from across the Midwest and around the world.

11

VOLUNTEERS

Early in Playhouse Square's history, ushers were paid a small sum primarily at the Palace Theater. Ushers were part of the experience of going out envisioned by Sam "Roxy" Rothafel as he was promoting large cathedral movie theaters. His idea was quickly picked up by Edward Albee through the Keith Circuit and Marcus Loew. Ushers at grand theaters were part of the elegance of going out on the town to see a silent movie or a vaudeville show. Howard Higley, longtime manager of the Allen Theater, began his career as a paid usher in the Palace. Higley and many others can trace their interests in theater back to time spent as ushers when Playhouse Square first opened and prior to the closings of all the theaters. John Kappan was a seventeen-year-old usher at the Palace in 1930, and when the Palace Theater reopened in 1988, he was an usher once again, this time as a volunteer.

Volunteers were the background help that reinvigorated Playhouse Square when Ray Shepardson first worked to save and reopen the theaters on Euclid Avenue. When Shepardson first worked at the Allen Theater to begin performances, he drew in a broad swath of young volunteers who contributed many hours. Some came from the efforts of Elaine Hadden and her contacts through the Junior League of Cleveland and their contacts to community business organizations. Some came from Cleveland State University, just down the street—energetic college students looking for a cause to support. Some, like fifteen-year-old Frank Dutton, were in high school and came down every day after school to help out.

Dutton remembers reading news articles about the closing and reopening of the Allen Theater and reports in the papers about whether the Playhouse

Square theaters would ever open again. His interest in working to make the community better brought him down to the Allen Theater on March 24, 1972. Meeting Ceil Hartman, then both a volunteer and a business manager employee, Dutton was invited to come back the following day to help out with the Richard Harris show. Shepardson, ever the invitational juggernaut, placed Frank in charge of the west mezzanine concession stand that evening. Dutton returned after school the following Monday to help with the cleanup, and he was hooked, eventually getting a part-time paid job for several years as the theaters struggled to gather momentum and support. The hook turned into a long-run interest in Playhouse Square, as he now documents events both historical and current on his blog.

There were high schoolers from Garfield Heights and a group of Lakewood folks—friends with Veralynne Bosko—who did much of the volunteer organizing in the early years. Bosko worked for a law firm located around Playhouse Square and may have been instrumental in helping Shepardson get the Playhouse Square Association started. Ushers at the early Allen concerts were all volunteers, and volunteers were used to sell items at the concession stands, clean up after guests and sweep the theater in preparation for the next night's show.

When Shepardson moved from the Allen Theater to prepare the lobby of the State Theater for the cabaret event of *Jacques Brel*, volunteers were instrumental in scraping old paint off woodwork, polishing marble, cleaning and setting up for the event. Volunteers helped collect tickets, clear plates after the dinner and usher patrons into and out of the lobby area from the entrance and exit points on East Seventeenth Street. What began as a necessity due to a lack of funds grew into a tradition at Playhouse Square that continues into the new century for the grand theaters.

The original dress code called for a tie and dress shirt for men, but the code was in no way standardized. In the late 1970s, Tom Rathburn volunteered with his wife. He was working as an accountant and already had spent time assisting at Berea Summer Theater, so his interest in theater was firmly grounded. He was typical of the volunteers who came down to assist patrons during this time. Volunteers had an interest or background in theater and wanted to support the newly formed Playhouse Square Association/Foundation as Shepardson was getting things off the ground. Rathburn continued as a volunteer until 1981, about the time that Larry Wilker arrived at Playhouse Square, and then he returned in the late 1980s, continuing today as the head of tour guides.

It was during Wilker's presidency that volunteers underwent another change. A suggestion was made that volunteers wear green jackets; however, John Hemsath remembers nixing that idea in favor of red. Redcoat volunteers were created. After the opening of the Ohio Theater, tour guides were instituted, and the Redcoats had a person formally placed in charge, Tom Alverson, also a volunteer. When John Kappan returned to Playhouse Square as a volunteer, there were nearly fourteen hundred Redcoats performing many jobs. Redcoats acted as ushers during performances, but behind the scenes they continued to print name tags, clean chandeliers and paint and polish.

Linda King was the front-of-the-house manager and manager of volunteers as a paid position. When the Palace Theater opened, putting three fully restored theaters into service, the need for volunteers increased. She was anticipating expanding the Redcoat stable to 2,000 volunteers. Where once 225 patrons were a very good audience, the Palace Theater now required 225 volunteers for a given show.

In 1988, the tour guides became more organized. Under the leadership of volunteers Bob Fahey, the tour guide originator, and later Bob Callester and Bob Herman, both tour guides, they researched the history of the theaters and compiled stories about the architecture, construction and restoration of each. A tour guide training book codified the stories and history. Tour guides went through an apprentice process, following other guides. They were reviewed as they took guests on tours. Tours were conducted on the first Saturday and Sunday of each month, and private tours were also held for groups and donors.

When the Allen Theater was being readied for opening *Forever Plaid*, it was volunteers who again scraped away years of grit and dirt. They removed seats and cleared debris. As Tom Rathburn recalls, the hard work was one of his strongest memories and most satisfying efforts as a volunteer.

As Playhouse Square enters the second century, there are still more than sixteen hundred volunteer Redcoats who usher and work behind the scenes to train other Redcoats, create name tags and preserve the history of the theaters. Many volunteers have thousands of hours of time logged at Playhouse Square. When asked why they put in the time, their answers range from "It reminds me of when I was young and went to the theaters downtown" to, "It is an opportunity to give back and support the city of Cleveland." The bottom line for most Redcoats is that theater is important and being a part of theater in Cleveland is worth supporting. Doing it for free is an act of joy.

12

THE FUTURE AND THE
NEXT ONE HUNDRED YEARS

ina Vernaci toured the Ohio and the yet-to-be-renovated State and Palace Theaters in 1984 with Larry Wilker as part of an interview for an intern job at Playhouse Square. The job was to last only about three months. Wilker could not promise anything beyond that, knowing that the financial footing of the foundation was tenuous. Vernaci accepted the offer and, like many others associated with Playhouse Square, stayed. Wilker identifies Vernaci as one of his best hires. In 2018, she assumed the role of president and CEO of Playhouse Square.

Vernaci's ascension to the top job came after thirty-four years of working through the steps at Playhouse Square. She helped grow Playhouse Square into a theater center and economic powerhouse that sees more than one million visitors a year. She is a member of the board for the Broadway League and the road vice-chair for the national trade association. She also served as a member of the Independent Presenters Network, an investment committee that helps produce touring shows. Her positions of leadership help to create influence and access for Cleveland's Playhouse Square. Vernaci guided Cleveland to a coveted three-week touring schedule for Broadway shows, opened up a secondary series titled the Key Bank Series, helped to establish a Broadway in Akron program and lands high-profile shows early in their touring life. Playhouse Square was one of a very few cities to host *Hamilton* for more than eight weeks, with a scheduled return performance run in the future.

Connections through the Broadway League led to a Disney link, in which Disney musicals such as *Aladdin* and *Frozen* were on the list for Cleveland's audiences. Vernaci carefully chooses performances, working to remain true to Playhouse Square's mission of providing entertainment for every taste.

Under her watchful eye, Playhouse Square is looking toward a bright future. Prior to the pandemic hitting all live performance venues, the Broadway series ticket subscription base rose to forty-six thousand members. Cleveland Play House was having a banner sellout season with increasing subscriptions, and Great Lakes Theater was providing innovative performances not just of Shakespeare but of musicals as well. The success and reputation of Playhouse Square creates a deep trust in the organization to present valued and varied entertainment options. Even though performances were canceled during most of the 2020 season and all of the 2020–21 season, Cleveland's subscribers donated their ticket costs to the foundation or did not drop their subscriptions. Trust and loyalty like that can only point to continued success.

The opening of the Lumen apartment complex across the street from the Conner Palace Theater enhances the neighborhood vibe around Playhouse Square. The Lumen will increase the number of full-time residents in the area. The Apartments at the Hanna, the Edge on Cleveland State

Restored auditorium of the Mimi Ohio Theater. *Photo from Redcoat Tour posting, 2019.*

Restored orchestra seating covering from the balcony of the Conner Palace Theater. *Author's photo, 2018.*

Restored auditorium of the Key Bank State Theater. *Photo from Redcoat Tour posting, 2019.*

University's campus and other university living spaces off Chester Avenue, combined with new housing options being constructed up Euclid Avenue in Cleveland, actually create the twenty-four/seven activity that Oliver Henkel and John Lewis imagined thirty years earlier.

When Playhouse Square first opened in 1921, the country was coming out of a global pandemic (the Spanish flu epidemic of 1918–20), and entertainment survived and thrived. Gina Vernaci sees no reason to be anything less than hopeful for the future. In an article in the *Cleveland Plain Dealer* in December 2020, she said:

> *Playhouse Square has faced many, many challenges in our history including the wrecking ball being out front. We do know how to rally. We are fortunate that there is a generous funding community in Northeast Ohio whose continued support will help keep our mission alive and Playhouse Square strong....We know that there's a demand on the other side.*

Gina Vernaci is correct that there is demand on the other side, and the theaters of Playhouse Square will continue to draw patrons to performances. Imagine one hundred years from now the awe that will be inspired as patrons enter the magnificent auditoriums, look up at the plastered ceilings, settle into their seats and disappear into the characters that present the story on stage. Imagine the views from theater stages, reflecting the glory of a time when deluxe movie and show palaces were built. The story of Playhouse Square is one of hardworking characters protecting magnificent theaters. It is a story of providing positive experiences to meet the demand on the other side. One hundred years from now, time will prove Gina Vernaci right.

BIBLIOGRAPHY

More than eight hundred articles from the *Cleveland Plain Dealer* were consulted for this book. As those articles are too numerous to cite here, readers can contact the author at mroutapublications@gmail.com for more information.

Croly, Herbert David. *Marcu Alonzo Hanna, His Life and Work*. New York: The MacMillan Company, 1912.

Dutka, Allen F. *Historic Movie Theaters of Downtown Cleveland*. Charleston, SC: The History Press, 2016.

Dutton, Frank. "Allen Theatre." *Frank's Place* (blog). April 1, 2016. https://frank-dutton.blogspot.com.

———. Interview and email exchange with author. February–March 2020.

———." "Jacques Brel Is Alive and Well and Living in Paris." *Frank's Place* (blog). April 18, 2013. https://frank-dutton.blogspot.com.

———. "Jacques Brel Is Alive and Well and Living in Paris." *Frank's Place* (blog). April 18, 2017. https://frank-dutton.blogspot.com.

———. "Loew's Ohio, Winter 1973." *Frank's Place* (blog). January 5, 2018. https://frank-dutton.blogspot.com.

———. "Playhouse Square Associaiton: The Early Years." *Frank's Place* (blog). April 16, 2014. https://frank-dutton.blogspot.com.

Einhouse, Tom, interview by Bridget Sekuterski, Cleveland Voices, 2005. https://clevelandvoices.org/items/show/1901.

Hall, Ben. *The Best Remaining Seats*. New York: Bramhall House, 1961.

Hemsath, John. Interview and email exchange with author. March 2020.

———. Interview by Andreana Somich. *Cleveland Voices*. 2006. https://clevelandvoices.org/items/show/1939.

Kennedy, Kathleen. *Playhouse Square "Redbook."* Cleveland: Playhouse Square Foundation, 1975.

Kennedy, Kathleen, and Jean Emser Schultz. *Playhouse Square, Cleveland: An Entertaining History: 1819 to the 21st Century.* Cleveland, OH: Playhouse Square Foundation, 2000.

Laurie, Joe, Jr. *Vaudeville: From Honkytonks to the Palace.* New York: Henry Holt and Company, 1953.

Rathburn, Thomas, interview by Bridget Sekuterski. Cleveland Voices. November 3, 2005. https://clevelandvoices.org/items/show/1891.

Segall, Gran. "Lannie Hadden, 88, Bubbly and Persuasive Civic Crusader, Died Friday." Cleveland.com. September 25, 2019. Accessed February 4, 2021. https://www.cleveland.com.

Sobel, Bernard. *A Pictorial History of Vaudeville.* New York: The Citadel Press. 1961.

Thinkmedia Studios. *Staging Success: The Playhouse Square Story.* PBS/WVIZ Public Broadcasting. https://vimeopro.com/thinkmediastudios/work/video/48975705.

Vacha, John. *From Broadway to Cleveland: A History of the Hanna Theatre.* Kent, OH: Kent State University Press, 2007.

———. *Showtime in Cleveland: The Rise of a Regional Theater Center.* Kent, OH: Kent State University Press, 2001.

Wilker, Lawrence. Interview with author, April 2020.

ABOUT THE AUTHOR

Michael R. Routa is a retired special education teacher, school administrator and adjunct university professor working for the Elyria City Schools and Ashland University. He grew up in the Cleveland area, graduated with bachelor's and master's degrees from Cleveland State University and a doctorate from Bowling Green State University. He completed research in the field of education and shared his findings at numerous conferences across the country. Upon retirement, he became a volunteer Redcoat at Playhouse Square and soon after was invited to be a tour guide. As a guide, he has the great opportunity to showcase Cleveland's wonderful theaters at Playhouse Square to visitors from across the country—theaters that should be seen to be fully appreciated. Michael is married and has one son.

Visit us at
www.historypress.com

www.ingramcontent.com/pod-product-compliance
Lightning Source LLC
Chambersburg PA
CBHW060345100426
42812CB00003B/1129